flex: Do Something Different

Also by the authors:

Love Not Smoking: Do Something Different

Do Something Different: The Journal

The No Diet Diet: Do Something Different
co-authored with Dr Danny Penman

Sheconomics
by Professor Karen J Pine and Simonne Gnessen

(Inner) FITness and the FIT Corporation
by Professor Ben (C) Fletcher and Bob Stead

flex:
Do Something Different

How to use the other 9/10ths of your personality

Professor Ben (C) Fletcher | Professor Karen J Pine

UNIVERSITY OF HERTFORDSHIRE PRESS

First published in Great Britain
in 2012 by:

University of Hertfordshire Press
College Lane
Hatfield
Hertfordshire
AL10 9AB
UK

British Library Cataloguing
in Publication Data

A catalogue record for this book is
available from the British Library
ISBN **978-1-907396-54-0**

Design by
Whiteing Design Partnership
Tel (01582) 792215
www.whiteingdesign.co.uk

Printed in Great Britain by
MPG Books Group Ltd

Preface

This book has a history. In the true spirit of **flex**, it is both old and new. Both mature and youthful. Many of the ideas in it stretch back, quite a way back. Even back to the times when Ben Fletcher had hair. Yes, they go back to Ben's post-Oxford days when he first researched why some individuals get stressed. And back to the birth of FIT Science to revisit some of the principles that Ben wrote about, with Bob Stead, in the book (*Inner) FITness & The FIT Corporation*. That book is no longer in print and in any case Ben had decided that it needed bringing up to date. So, in a sense, this is the new and improved FIT handbook. But it is also so much more than that.

About the time that he realised FIT needed revamping and revitalising, bringing new thoughts to bear on the original theories, Ben had also started to express those ideas in a new, more powerful (some would say more accessible) format. That was probably from 2004 onwards, when he started working with his wife Karen Pine. Together they are the proud 'parents' of the Do Something Different approach that makes up much of this book. That's why the voice in the book shifts from 'I' to 'we' at times. The 'I' is Ben, expounding old and new ideas and putting them into his voice. The 'we' is the product of that thinking and the work of Ben and Karen together. Ultimately, though, Ben and Karen are a partnership, in life and in work, sharing the same views and speaking with one voice.

How to use this book

There are four sections to this book. They do have a sequence to them but we have tried to include many smaller sub-sections for the reader who prefers to dip in and out. At the end of each of the four main sections we give you ways to put the ideas into practice – a '**flex** in action' section. As the theory unfolds you'll see how **flex** is all about expanding your world and making full use of your personality, since most of us are driven by habit and use just a fraction of our potential. The more you can put the **flex** technique – i.e. Do Something Different (DSD) – into practice, the more you will experience for yourself the worlds it can open up for you.

The first section explains why we are all so habitual and how the nature of the human brain drives us towards repetitive thoughts and behaviours. And why these aren't always good for us. At the end of that section you can test, with the habit-rater, how habitual you are (you may be surprised since most of us are unaware of this limitation). Then you can get a first taste of the Do Something Different technique by trying some simple DSDs in your daily life, as a way of breaking free of some of your simplest habits. The DSDs are simple and fun yet also enlightening and will prepare you for the next section, Section 2.

This describes how the idea of behavioural flexibility came about and why it is so critical to all aspects of our lives. And how it impacts on our physical and mental health and well-being. Section 2 concludes with the behaviour-rater – a quick assessment of your own behavioural repertoire – and then dozens of practical ways in which you can expand yourself and really enjoy the full experience of **flex**, by waking up the hitherto unused parts of your personality.

In Section 3 we present the greater goal of **flex** – personal coherence – and how this can move you to function at the optimal level. That involves having all parts of your life in alignment with each other, creating a coherent and harmonious way of living. After Section 3 you'll find another self-assessment tool, this time the coherence-rater, to give you insight into where you can enhance your own personal coherence. This is followed by several projects to work on coherence and expand your own life.

Finally, Section 4 takes **flex** beyond the individual and argues for the need to move towards a coherent and flexible world.

Contents

Section 2 – Behavioural flexibility

Section 3 – Doing something different, personal coherence and decision-making

Section 4 – Global issues and flex

Appendix

1

Section 1:
The human habit machine

1. How many kinds of people are there?

This may seem an inauspicious beginning but a pivotal point in my academic career happened in a Chinese restaurant near Hatfield, not far from where I was working at the University of Hertfordshire. It was the late 1970s. The waiter was young and eager. He made polite conversation while serving us and he found out that I was a psychologist. When I was paying the bill, he asked if I would mind answering a question for him. I said I would if I could. His question has stayed with me in the decades since because it encapsulates a common misconception about people.

The waiter asked me this:
'How many kinds of people are there?'

I'll tell you the answer I gave him in due course. But I did not shy away from the question. It would have been easy to sidestep it by saying something like, 'It depends what you mean' or 'What definition of "kinds" do you have in mind?' (Psychologists always carry a whole armoury of sidestepping statements around with them.) After a little discussion, though, I knew exactly what he meant. It all became clear when the word 'personality' cropped up.

What is a reasonable answer? Given that we are all individuals, perhaps it could have been, *'As many kinds as there are people in the world.'* Or even a very large number since we are all individuals. But that does not seem to be the case. Psychologists believe they have the answer to how many kinds of people there are because, in principle, people have personalities that fit into certain categories. Psychologists can, by various ways and means, fit them into a finite number of categories – usually described by between two and five personality traits. For example, in the 'big five' these are agreeableness, conscientiousness, extroversion, neuroticism and openness to experience.

Why should this be so? Humans are habit machines and they tend to behave predictably. People tend to behave the same in different situations.

It seems safe to say that, if we know someone, we've a good idea of what to expect of them. We often say, 'Oh, that's just typical of Bill.' Or, 'I might have known Jenny would say that!' In fact, we can even figure out something about a person we *don't* know very well. Just being told about 'Simon, who wears lizard skin shoes,' might lead you to make certain assumptions about the type of person Simon is. Or hearing that 'Lucy reacted very badly to the criticism' would help you predict how she would respond to a cutting remark in the future.

So my answer to the waiter's question, 'How many kinds of people are there?' at that time led me to tell him that empirical psychological research had come up with five 'big' personality traits. That's what my academic studies had taught me. But I remember also questioning the sense of dividing personality into five categories. It seemed as absurd to me as the twelve astrological signs of horoscopes. His question led me to ponder why people should be categorised. Might they not become imprisoned by the category they were assigned to? Wouldn't it be more important to be able to behave in the best and most appropriate way as required by the situation? Like a tree that bends with the wind, to have a fluid and flexible personality that could flex according to need?

I told the waiter I found the 'big five' strange and I did not know why it was such a popular idea. And I also began to suspect that assigning people to a personality type might not be such a good thing because of the dangers of it becoming self-limiting. Couldn't people benefit from having a personality that was more dynamic and even allowed them to move between the types if circumstances required it?

Today I would have told him about **flex**.

2. The personality trap

On the face of it, it just doesn't make sense for a person to behave the same way in all types of different situations. The world is constantly changing, families are dynamic, people die, jobs change or are lost, finances grow and shrink and these changes call for adaptability and different responses. The more fixed a person's personality is, the harder they'll find it to adapt to the new. The more vulnerable they will be to stress.

Life is so varied and so changeable that there isn't one personality 'type' suited to it. How can a person make the most of what life throws at them if they have fixed ways of being? If they approach today's situations with yesterday's strategies? No wonder people often commit faux pas, make fools of themselves, feel overwhelmed or out of their depth. How can we develop and grow unless we learn from the old and adapt our wisdom to the new? People's failure to do so explains a whole catalogue of missed opportunities, misunderstandings and dysfunction.

And yet most humans are predictable in the extreme. Most have a limited repertoire of fairly predictable behaviours. That's why psychologists can assign them a personality category. Yet many people are vain enough – some would even say deluded enough – to believe, when they reflect on something they have done, that they acted out of choice. Moreover, that they were able to put their personality aside for a moment and act in the 'best' way. They would say that they meant to take the course of action they did and that there was some careful consideration involved.

Even though anyone who knew them could have predicted they would behave as they did.

The rather unpalatable truth is that most of our seemingly conscious intentions are just illusions. Our past habits, which make up our personality, hijack our ability to exercise free will or act differently. They inhibit awareness and take the decision out of our hands. Many intentions to act, or choices, are not the result of having judged the situation and made a conscious choice. They are more likely to spring from past behavioural patterns.

From our autopilot. We do what we do in a new situation because we did that kind of thing in the past. But if we cannot **flex** ourselves, we will become prisoners of our personality.

Extroversion–introversion is one of the 'big five' personality traits. Yet consider for a moment the extrovert who is the life and soul of the party and happy being the centre of attention. His extroversion is not always an asset. In fact it becomes a handicap when he's forced to have a quiet night in, or on a visit to his girlfriend's sombre parents. The introvert on the other hand may cling to the walls at a wild party, but knows how to enjoy his own company or that of more serious folk. A person who can **flex**, using extroversion and introversion traits appropriately, is equally comfortable in either context. His personality does not alienate him from any corner of the world.

This is why we refer to the 'personality trap'. It may keep us from doing the best for ourselves, from coping with all facets of our world, and we'll talk more about that later. But you may be thinking that having a definite personality has some advantages too. And indeed it does. We like to be seen to be consistent. People like to feel they know us and know what to expect from us. They like to be able to label us and put us in a box. That predictability – our personality – becomes our personal trademark. It defines who we are and is our behavioural footprint on the world. There are personal and social benefits, for ourselves and others, from being consistent in how we behave. It is also a highly energy-efficient way for the human system to operate, as we'll see in the next section.

3. People on autopilot

When a pilot switches his controls to autopilot he can relax a little. He no longer needs to be hyper-attentive to all the aircraft's operations. As we go about our daily life we too can switch our operating system to autopilot. This means we don't have to think too much and so we reduce the demands on our cognitive and processing systems. We can probably spend around 90 per cent of our day in this state. Going through the motions. Doing what we usually do. Trotting out the same well-worn sayings. I often refer to it as 'sleeping with our eyes open'. It would be too demanding, even exhausting, to stay alert and conscious of everything we do and think every second of the day. Imagine contemplating every thought you had, every sensation you experienced and every breath you took from the moment you awoke. You'd never get out of bed. A simple question like 'How are you?' would require agonising self-examination, comparisons and introspection. Every decision would be torturous. As well as being personally stressful, this would simply bamboozle your brain. The brain is hard-wired precisely to avoid this overload by operating on the efficiency principle. It creates automaticity to stop us over-thinking.

Have you ever been driving somewhere and found you've taken your usual route to work instead of where you were meant to be driving to? Or found yourself putting sugar in your partner's tea when you know they have given up? Or throwing rubbish into a wastepaper bin that has been moved? These all demonstrate how unconscious and automatic much of our behaviour is when we are operating 'efficiently' or without thought.

So this efficiency principle has a cost. There's a downside to being able to assign so much of living to an automatic pilot and not just in the errors described above. Sure, efficiency and automaticity conserve our brain's valuable resources. And it may be handy for people to know how we're likely to react in given situations. To know, for example, that if we said we would arrive at eight o'clock, we will do so. Or that if asked to treat something in confidence we can be relied on not to blab. But this has to be weighed against the times when doing what we always do leads us to act without thinking. To let our personality take over. To produce an automatic response to a situation where another, more considered reaction would have been more appropriate. To use just 1/10th of our potential personality.

Automaticity – being at the mercy of our narrow personality – means there will be new experiences that we try to solve with old models. Our constantly changing life will present us with opportunities that we will fail to notice. Decisions made when we are on autopilot will not always be the right ones. There will be unguarded occasions when our mindlessness allows others to manipulate us for their own ends. Unless we can **flex** we will fail to act upon life as it is in this very moment.

4. flexing

flex is about taking charge of ourselves when it is important. It's about not giving ourselves over to automaticity. It's about avoiding the personality trap. When we **flex** we do not lose ourselves but can adapt to what is happening in the moment.

One way to consider the need to **flex** comes from understanding the enormous costs to the individual of being too habitual. I'll go into that more later. But I also have a more positive motivation for introducing the benefits of **flex**. The waiter in the Chinese restaurant prompted me to develop a new notion about personality.

I believe that we all have the capacity to be different people. In fact, the extent of our success in life will depend on the extent to which we develop that capacity. By that I do not mean being a charlatan or a fake individual. I mean a person making the most of every situation, the familiar and the new, by acting with integrity for the good of themselves and others.

We use only a fraction of our potential personality. We have a toolkit full of useful behaviours, yet repeatedly pull out the same one. We have myriad ways of reacting to situations, yet we do as we have always done. As long as we do this there will be a mismatch between life's conditions and the strategies we use to cope with them. About 9/10ths of our tools for life are lying, gathering dust, in our brain's toolbox.

We have seen repeatedly how **flex** is the key to overcoming many of the problems and struggles that people face. It does this by first helping people break the stranglehold of habits and automaticity. There may be only one world 'out there' but in practice everyone's experience of the world varies enormously. The reason for this difference lies in the very different capacities of individuals to make the most of what life brings. Some of these differences we can do little or nothing about – our genes and our upbringing, for example. But we do have an enormously powerful tool at our disposal to change the reactions and responses of those around us – how we behave.

Take two people who each encounter the same problem in their life. One may view it as a personal disaster, the other as a challenge. Their reaction will determine how they respond, the first being beaten down by the problem and the second fired up to overcome it. **flex** is about understanding that we all have those choices. Whoever we are and whatever our background. And it's about knowing that when we choose a *different* behaviour, from the unused 9/10ths of our personality, it brings about a totally different effect in both us and others.

If we **flex** we can change and expand our world. And with a little conscious effort we have the capacity to dramatically alter the world we live in. **flex** is world-altering in this sense.

We all have the capacity to be different people. We limit our life by being only ourselves, by using just 1/10th of our personality.

5. People shrink their worlds

Our automatic habits of thought and action lead us to create a world for ourselves that is much smaller than it needs to be. I would even go so far as to say that some people shrink their worlds so much that they create problems and difficulties for themselves. Life produces struggles, demands and worries for us all, of course. But some people attract problems by their behaviours and habits. Their trials and tribulations come in all forms. Unwanted addictions, being overweight or stressed, being unloved, not getting on in life and so on. It's tempting to assume that the person who's struggling is a victim of circumstances. Some unfortunate people undoubtedly are. But, more often than not, people are as much a victim of their own habits, repetitive patterns and their inability to yield and **flex** themselves.

You have probably noticed, for example, that as some people get older their world seems to contract, to get smaller. Some older people seem less tolerant; they are more resistant to change and less open to new things. They will often say that they don't like change or that they are set in their ways. This is because, by consistently repeating the same patterns of behaviour, their thoughts and actions have become more automated and less conscious. Their world has become smaller in a real sense. No wonder that time flies as we get older, as more and more is done automatically. Ageing is in some ways a self-fulfilling process. It does not have to be like that. Modern medicine now increasingly recognises the value of getting older people to expand their world. They are urged to try new things – take up dancing, get a dog, rent an allotment – to increase their social networks and stay physically and mentally active. Whether this will ward off Alzheimer's is a question for the gerontologists, but it will make life more fun and more rewarding.

6. We are all capable of change

In this book we will show you how being able to **flex** could enrich your old age, beat stress, bring you loving relationships and open your mind to opportunities that might otherwise pass you by. We will help you to put it into practice with examples and practical guidance. Meanwhile, there is another reason I urge you to consider the benefits of **flex**.

In general, I have found that the differences between people in terms of the things about them that are alterable are far greater and more important than the differences between them in terms of the parts that are fixed or harder to change (perhaps their IQ, educational history, genes or age). We cannot change the structural things, but we do have the capability to change many fluid aspects of our own behaviours and personality traits. You no doubt know two people who are of the same chronological age, but one thinks like an energetic teenager and the other has a decaying mindset. How does that happen? It isn't all fixed and predetermined. Many characteristics we hold are changeable, even though it may not seem so because they have become habitual. We can do something about so many facets of who we are. That is another reason for **flex**.

Many people find change difficult. In my personal and professional life I have seen countless examples of people honestly saying one thing yet doing another. An example might be the man who says he wishes to lose weight but reaches for a second helping of dessert. The girl who orders a giant-sized hamburger and a 'diet' cola. The woman who wants to take up jogging but says she can't give up smoking. People struggle, it seems, even to make the changes that they know would transform their lives. Then there are people who repeat the same mistakes and appear not to notice, driven as they are by their habitual behaviour patterns. The man who pays his wife no attention, yet complains that she 'nags'. The woman who constantly breaks arrangements and wonders why her friends avoid her.

Some people have enormous energy but it is wrongly channelled; others have intentions that are good but behaviours that do them harm.

Everywhere there are people who stress themselves, people stuck in a rut, people who fail to spot the mistakes in what they do and say (yet they would notice them in others), people who do not learn from their mistakes, and people bound by habits of thinking and behaviour. We all do these things to a greater or lesser degree. We can all benefit from being able to make small changes, if we only knew where and how. Later in this book we'll describe the techniques we've used to help those who want to overcome life's challenges, to become more coherent, and to have better relationships and altogether more fulfilling lives. At the very core of these techniques lies the ability to **flex**.

7. Shaping a life

I am a product of my past. My genes from my parents were perhaps of dubious quality. They both died young. My dad was a taciturn bricklayer who worked seven days most weeks. Mum was a bit of a nervous wreck who had to undergo electro-convulsive therapy when I was about five years old. She went through enormous struggles to manage money and as a young boy I lived in constant fear of the bailiff or debt collector who made a point of calling when my dad got home from work. Mum's life was unrelentingly hard and she wasn't as good as she thought at keeping a lid on the mess. When I had just started school I became very ill. I had to stay at home in bed for a considerable period of time. Mum told me I had contracted – and finally overcome – polio. It wasn't until I was in my fifties and had cause to look at my medical records that I learnt the 'polio' was in fact 'dysentery', a disease frequently associated with poor sanitation. She had to make the story up to protect herself, I guess. It stuck!

My upbringing was fine but pretty basic in many ways and compared to many it did have shortcomings. Being in a large family meant I had enough brothers to play football, without having to rely on finding other kids. That was good. But it wasn't a loving family environment, although neither was it abusive. My parents simply did what they knew. OK, so my childhood had some negatives for me but that can be the nature of growing up. Good things have bad sides and bad things have good. I vividly remember the sinking feeling and fear I had once when I was about ten years old. I received a letter saying I was going to be taken to court because I had not paid for stamps I had sent for 'on approval'. I knew I had to deal with that myself and so I wrote them a letter saying I would pay for them soon. I couldn't impose more worries on mum, even though she had told me I could have the stamps – probably in a moment of weakness. From a very young age I was acutely aware that she had a raw deal and that her daily life was full of suffering. So I just learned to deal with all kinds of problems myself. I privately worked out the best solutions I could without ever troubling my parents. But I couldn't solve everything. For example, when I was about sixteen I can remember wondering how girlfriends would react to me (and whether they might reject me) when they found out where I lived. So my childhood wasn't all plain sailing and there were certainly 'scars' that remained, once I had grown up.

But, looking back, I realise my parents gave me a jewel that is so often lacking in current parental practices (particularly among the over-involved middle classes). My parents' preoccupation with the toils of daily living meant they left me to work out for myself how to shape a life. They simply didn't have the resources, time or energy to intervene. I had to discover, sometimes the hard way, how to make decisions. I had to be totally self-led and self-sufficient. No one ever offered me advice or guidance, or said to me 'do this', 'don't do that', 'you can't' or 'this is how to behave'. As a result I learned how to shape life for myself and worked out how to be. Of course that wasn't always easy and some would say that's finding out the hard way, because I didn't know the rules, or what works, or what others do or expect. I may have made mistakes along the way but the positive outcome is that I certainly became the architect and designer of my own life. I learned that we can shape the way we live and the way we are. We can act in the world rather than be acted upon. A most valuable lesson.

8. Why the past doesn't help our future

I've told you a little of my unusual past but only to illustrate a skill I learned from it. I certainly don't hold on to the past or hark back to it at all. A critical part of making the most of life, and shaping it, means taking the opportunities that come your way. I have found that if I make the most of these opportunities, tomorrow brings with it even more options and choices for me – the future is less uncertain because I am influencing it today. But there is a golden rule that I have found it essential to live by. That golden rule is the core message of this book – it is the necessity to **flex**. That means that on my personal journey through life I have always tried to:

- change my mind should the evidence require it
- behave differently to make the most of an opportunity
- accept there are many things I know little about, but to be open enough to try them
- tolerate uncertainty and
- tolerate ambiguity.

An aspect of this is not using yesterday's solutions to deal with today's problems. Because I know the problems I will be faced with today are likely to be inherently different from those I have faced before. I may not always perceive it that way but I have always recognised that the world changes constantly and so must I.

Models of the past are rarely of any use in the present. That is what **flex** is all about – having the ability to notice when the current situation needs a non-habitual response. **flex** is about using all the tools in your toolbox. Imagine a craftsman who has to fix all kinds of objects and craft a range of artefacts. If every time he reached into his toolbox he pulled out a hammer, what a poor job he would make of the tasks that faced him. Yet every day people walk around with well-stocked toolboxes and all they use is a hammer. And they shrink their worlds because when all you have is a hammer everything looks like a nail.

To put this another way – they are failing to use the other 9/10ths of their personality.

I've already mentioned that habits and natural tendencies can have some use. But they are dangerous allies when they hijack your decisions and blind you to alternatives and opportunities for development. Let me explain further.

Doubtless we all agree that the world is 'out there' and objective in some important sense (e.g. it is independent of us). Philosophers have debated this for centuries. But for me at any rate I believe we all share a physical world; I think that is a truth. It is a fact. It is real. We all live in the world. However, people often mistake their subjective perception of the world for objective reality and this causes all sorts of problems.

Our worlds are very different but often we do not realise that. We see things in different ways. No two people's views of an event are the same. Witnesses of the same crime frequently, to the frustration of police officers, give completely different versions of what 'happened'. Our perspective feels as if it is the objective world. We need to be self-responsible so we can determine and shape the narrative we live our own life by. If we believe that gods and demons can shape it, or that luck and fate will intervene, then it will be so. I have tried to live my life by taking charge of what happens, even though sometimes I have been at best a poor director, and at other times an apparent victim of circumstance, such as an impoverished childhood. Yes, events have sometimes seemed to conspire against me, for example, losing both my parents early in life, but I have still lived with the belief that I alone was responsible for how things turned out. If it is a false belief, I cannot see that it is a harmful one. In fact, I have probably never actually been a victim of circumstance, however it seemed at the time – I have been a victim only of myself and my level of self-responsibility.

So the most important person to convince is yourself.

9. We are all habit machines

Our brains are hard-wired to develop habits. Habits and the brain's autopilot facility save energy. The brain is only 2 per cent of our body weight but consumes 20 per cent of our energy resources. So it is expensive to run in terms of resources and operates on an efficiency principle. It will always take shortcuts based on what it already knows or has done before. That is just a natural part of the human condition and is true of us all. Of course our habits have evolved because they are efficient in helping us to size up the world, to warn us of danger and to allow us to make decisions without effort. Yet we can operate consciously too. We do not have to be habit-driven all the time. But often people fall back on using their habits instead of examining their decisions and behaviours to see if they are optimal. That leads them into all kinds of difficulties.

In fact we are much more habitual than we would like to believe. To develop, to get the most from life, to be happy and fulfilled, to be fully rounded human beings, we need to examine not only how habitual we are, but which habits we have acquired. Because we see the world through these habits. They distort, warp, disguise and shape what we think and see. We see things from only our narrow perspective and behave accordingly. Much may be gained by realising that we have shaped our own worlds with the constraints of these habits and that things could be very different. We tend to make the world much smaller than it can be. That is why different people see different things in the same situation. That is why what appears to be so obvious and objective to us is often perceived so differently by another. That is why we have conflicts, both within ourselves and with others. Our habits filter the world; they don't just change how we behave in it.

10. Habits come in many forms

Every second the senses are bombarded with ten to twelve million bits of information to process. We can only process about fifty bits of information a second. Hence the need to automatise much of the process and to develop habits in many forms.

Habits of *perception* make sense of the world for us and organise incoming information quickly and efficiently. The brain is adept at sense-making. It can fill in gaps and recognise patterns using only limited perceptual information. Habits of *thinking* are mental shortcuts. We can use intelligent guesswork without putting in too much mental effort. Rules of thumb can be drawn from our experience and we can quickly categorise something that's new on the basis of our stored knowledge.

Habits of *attitude* mean we do not need to contemplate the nuances of much that we come into contact with. We may see and process according to what we think we know, rather than based on the evidence before us. Unfortunately this is where our most unsavoury habits can grow, in the form of prejudices and biases.

Habits of *behaviour* remove the need to consider everything that we do. Reaching for a seat belt whenever I get into the car is a behaviour that I am happy to have automated. So habits can be very effective. Indeed, they are the reason we manage so well on autopilot. They are the reason we can drive, play sports, get dressed in the dark, and do many things at once. They explain why we can survive in a highly complex world without being overwhelmed by choices. Habits may well even be responsible for why we see the world in a shared way despite the fact that our viewpoints are all so different.

But.

But.

But these habits also mean we spend 90 per cent of our waking time on autopilot. We sleep with our eyes open. Our brain – which apparently gives us a special place in the animal kingdom because it allows cognate thought – likes to fool us into thinking that we control ourselves. The conscious thoughts generated by our frontal lobes chug away in happy ignorance of the fact that much of our behaviour is going on under the control of the faster, primitive parts of the brain. Yes, habits rob us of detail and difference. Habits make us see different things in the same way and so are responsible for us often missing what we are not looking for, even if that would be really useful for us. People don't spot the gorilla let alone dare to mention the elephant in the room! Much of the time this may not have disastrous consequences. After all we don't miss what we do not know or see. But there are many situations when we would be better off if we 'took charge' of ourselves and woke up to the present reality. These include:

- when our habits make us miss things that would be good for us
- when we fail to make the most of a situation because we treat it as similar to previous ones (when it is not)
- if we need to stop or modify an unwanted behaviour
  (e.g. being too assertive, hostile, fearful, irritable, etc.)
- if we wish to give up something we are addicted or
  habituated to (alcohol, smoking, over-eating, shopping, etc.) and
- if we need to change for the better in any way.

11. The myth of willpower

Habits are by their very nature tough, resilient and hard to crack. That is a simple fact, yet most behaviour change techniques simply ignore it. It is assumed that people find it hard to change because they do not have enough 'willpower'. New Year's resolutions are abandoned before the Christmas decorations are down, people 'fall off the wagon' and diets get dumped regularly. People, it seems, simply cannot summon enough effort to improve their life. In reality, as soon as a person's guard is down, their attention wanders, or they bump up against an old habit trigger, and the autopilot nips in and retakes control. Then 'willpower' doesn't stand a chance. Sometimes, if the person is not really committed to change, or is just too tired, habits will regain control very quickly. Research has suggested that willpower uses brain food – it soaks up a lot of our energy. It has also been described as a limited resource that tires like a muscle. In other words, it is not much help to us when we want to make positive changes in our lives. When we want to defeat the pull of habits, it regularly lets us down. In fact, we would go so far as to say there is no such thing as willpower. It is based on an illusory sense of control. One that for a short and fleeting moment fools us into feeling we are in charge of ourselves. But then it is quickly gone, leaving us with little more than a sense of failure. Behaviour-change techniques need to stop trying to harness non-existent willpower and address what really stands in the person's way: their habits.

12. Becoming habit-free

Behaviour-change theorists tend to assume that people can get a grip on themselves and invoke that mysterious force called willpower. By really focusing on what they want, they assume people make certain targeted changes, and of course some do. Perhaps yoga might help us reorient and de-stress. Time management would prevent us from clogging up our lives with the irrelevant. Therapy would give us an understanding of where things had gone wrong in the past so that we could move on. Government initiatives to make us healthier and have better lifestyles work hard at educating us. They tell us what we should do that is good for us. Eat five fruit and veg a day, they say. Exercise for thirty minutes five times a week. Drink only so many units of alcohol. Attempts to fill us with information, education or incentives naively assume that people will willingly take their messages on board and then act in ways that reflect their best interests. So, according to this model, we are ignorant and just need be told what to do and then, miraculously, we will make the right changes. Most of us don't.

Anyone can see the nonsense in this. The obesity problem grows despite the emphasis on the need for a healthy diet. Smokers continue to light up from packets plastered with death warnings. Most dieters I have met are expert calorie counters but are still overweight. They know what they should and should not eat. They just cannot do it. We all have behaviours and thoughts we know are not good, we know what we should do, but we continually fail to do it. Change is not tackled by educating people; it is brought about by **flex**ing people.

13. Inertia and the status quo bias

What if people think they are fine as they are? Surely personal development should be a matter of personal choice? Some people cannot see the need to change, either personally, or for the benefit of others. Some have religious beliefs that say we have been made the way we are for a purpose. Some are too lazy. Some are too depressed to try. I have often found that the people who say they do not need to change are the ones in greatest need. They are often the people who are stress carriers (they cause stress in others but are fine themselves) or who lack self-insight, or whose behaviours damage others (often the ones they say they love). Yes, there are successful people too who say what they did worked for them, so why change? They think they have a unique formula for their success. However, there is no logic or sense in ignoring alternatives, or in being closed to possibilities. Ignorance and prejudice grow out of this kind of narrow-mindedness. Why dismiss an option that might be worth considering as potentially good for you? Being blind to possibility and personal growth is self-limiting. OK, so you might be fine today, but things don't stay the same – new behaviours become necessary, the world changes, different mindsets will constantly rise up and challenge you. You have to be open and ready.

There is another much stronger and more compelling reason for being open to alternatives. Consider whether there is an area of *your* life that is not as perfect as you would like it to be. We can almost guarantee that if you do nothing it will not improve. If you carry on in the same way, nothing will change. Einstein defined insanity as doing the same thing over and over again and expecting a different outcome. Yet how often do we wish things were different but do nothing to bring about changes? Isn't it madness to want something different but to continue to do the same? That is a key point but one that's often overlooked. We are taught by evolutionary theory that creatures who fail to adapt perish. It is the same for humans. We need to **flex** to thrive.

14. The pull of the past

A commonly held view is that problems can be overcome – and personal development progress – by looking into the past. Many people have a strong affinity with the past and especially with their own past. People usually think – quite erroneously in my view – that they know quite a bit about it too. We could argue about that. People know things from their viewpoint better than anyone else, but there are many other viewpoints. Our personal narratives can be shaped – and distorted – by the passing of time, by other people and by intervening events. People are very attracted to the idea that the past is the 'cause' of how they are today. They underestimate the extent to which our natural tendencies and personality contribute to where we are. These are, in fact, the most likely causes of our current issues and problems. Not our past. Our past may have shaped us. The more traumatic or abusive it was the greater our tendency to believe this. But – and this flies in the face of psychoanalysis and many psychotherapies – I believe *solutions do not come from an analysis of the past*. Nor does change happen naturally in a habit machine such as ourselves.

Our habits and natural tendencies account for why our past seems to stick to us very easily without the effort of will. This 'stickiness' is very difficult to shake off even when we need to, because many forces operate to maintain our natural inertial path. These include:

- genetic make-up
- parental upbringing
- past experiences and learning
- social pressures and the need to conform
- needs and wants for things and status
- demands of work and work colleagues and
- demands in our immediate environment.

These are all inertial or habit forces that conspire to keep us the way we were, largely independently of what is good or right for us. They are 'current self' cement. Or concrete boots slowing down the journey towards a different future self. If we do not **flex** away from them we can end up getting the opposite of what we want or risk making the present become permanent.

15. Shaping a new self

Who are you? Who am I? Perhaps we are only the sum of our genes, biology, upbringing and experiences. This would explain why we try to keep a strong grip on this container of the past. We have a tendency to believe it does define our 'selves'. We are probably programmed to defend it and not to move on because – in some sense – that means killing the current self. The alternative is to change our own habit machine and replace those natural tendencies with a different and more appropriate set of thoughts and behaviours; to construct almost a new 'self'. I stand by my assertion that if there is any fundamental difference between us and the rest of the animal kingdom it is apparent in how we develop ourselves independently of, and far beyond, our basic animalism. We can have more control over our own destiny than we often realise. And the litmus test of this is in our facility to shape a new self from past-driven natural tendencies.

flex is a proof of that personal control and the special position of being a human animal. **flex** is about:

- monitoring our existence and adapting to the subtle variations that we perceive
- hijacking our own habit machines to shape a better world
- putting the individual in control and
- abandoning notions of past, luck and limits, and replacing them with the potential and the positive.

The later sections of this book show you how we managed to find an easy way for people to do this. How people achieved changes in areas where they had failed repeatedly before. How some experienced life-changing transformations.

16. Show me a stressed person and I'll show you a habit machine

I have been researching occupational stress for over thirty years. In 1991 I wrote a book called *Work, Stress, Disease, and Life Expectancy*. Many tens of thousands of studies had tried to show that stress caused ill health and shortened life expectancy. I concluded that the term 'stress' is unhelpful and virtually meaningless because it encompasses all sorts of ways of defining 'stress' from the positively good to the definitely dangerous.

Nowadays very few people work in psychologically toxic environments, even though that may not be how it feels to many. People feel their work is stressful because they have got into the habit of attributing negative feelings to things outside themselves. For example, they blame the management, shortage of resources or the inefficiency of colleagues. My research on work stress showed that what one person thought was 'stressful' another person was energised by, or another did not notice at all. This difference between people seemed to be the key to tackling stress. It suggested to me that changing the work environment would have very little effect. The person is where stress resides and where change has to be targeted. I now know that helping the person to **flex** will empower them to cope better with their work and their life. I know that stress is often the consequence of having rigid behaviours and habits.

I have held positions of considerable responsibility and had jobs in senior management that some people would find stressful. I have been able to see how demands placed upon me might be construed as stressful by others. I have had bosses with whom I have had to behave in different ways, to accommodate their different styles, whims and predilections. Had I not been able to **flex** myself, their foibles, habits and even unreasonable demands would have stressed me. But I found I could subtly change *their* behaviour by adapting how I responded. By **flex**ing I could de-stress the situation and cope with many significant managerial predicaments, knowing when to be assertive and when to back down, for example, or understanding on which occasions it is important to give your boss public support, and when not to.

Or knowing when and when not to involve others in decision-making and knowing when to diffuse a situation with humour, and when gravitas is called for. Similarly I have made a point of empowering others to take more responsibility, to teach themselves to operate with awareness and to allow them the freedom to learn and to respond. So my job has been made even less stressful by developing and being tolerant of the range of different personal strengths of my team. I hope too that I have shown by my own behaviour that there are many alternative ways, flexible ways, of approaching a situation instead of being a habit machine.

17. Small changes, big consequences

What is responsible for the differences in how people respond to their environment? As an undergraduate at Keele University I came across René Thom's Cusp Catastrophe Theorem. This preceded Chaos Theory, which people are now fond of applying to management, or as a way of understanding organisations or predicting stock market performance. It is akin to what Malcolm Gladwell calls 'Tipping Points' – how small changes, often imperceptible, can make a big difference.

The essence of Thom's Theory is that discontinuity (catastrophe) in a system can sometimes happen if the system cannot cope with or absorb the stresses it is placed under. This brings about a new state without a route back to the old state. Push a bottle until it falls and you cannot push it back. When a system has flipped it cannot return to its original state. This explains why certain experiences can have lasting effects on some people and not others. What causes the system to flip (or the person to undergo a change in state) may have little to do with the experience itself but have more to do with the state of the person at the time. That is how an apparently innocuous event can be catastrophic for one person and virtually inconsequential for another and why we cannot easily erase some experiences. Just as we cannot suppress thinking about a white bear if told not to think of one, we cannot forget traumatic events (whether or not others would find them traumatic). Many problems cannot just be unlearned; there is no going back to the original state. One of the benefits of **flex** is that it enlarges the system's capacity to absorb and respond to events, without tipping over into catastrophe. In effect **flex** inoculates the person against catastrophe. It expands them beyond just operating with 1/10th of their potential system.

The theory also enlightens us as to why many apparently new experiences are treated as if they are ones we have experienced before. A person who has not learned to **flex**, whose system is narrow and constrained, will make the new appear old by their habits of thinking and behaviour. They will see the new through old eyes and may lack the responses needed to defuse catastrophe (the other 9/10ths). That is the power – and the inherent danger – of the habit machine we have met earlier on these pages. Treating the new as if it were the old has another negative consequence. Life will appear less rich and more repetitive (yet with more apparently 'damaging' events).

I went on to do a doctorate in the Department of Experimental Psychology at Oxford University on how we categorise and prejudge detail in our perceptual and decision-making domains. Later I went to work for the Medical Research Council Social and Applied Psychology Unit at Sheffield University (now the Institute of Work Psychology) with Dr Roy Payne on work stress.

Roy had developed the Demands–Supports–Constraints model of work stress. We tested predictions of this model on teachers and managers. We were trying to understand why demands in the workplace didn't account for the negative outcomes that people felt. It was clear to me then that the differences between people doing the same job are much greater than the differences between jobs. For example, there is a great deal in common between the jobs of line managers in a large organisation. Yet the way individuals view and respond to the demands of the job vary enormously.

There was another aspect of my work that became formative for FIT Science and **flex**. In my book *Work, Stress, Disease, and Life Expectancy* I put forward a catastrophe framework for stress. Thom and his catastrophe theory had been incubating in my mind all those years. The model explained why stressed people see the world very differently from unstressed people. They may be exposed to the same stressors in the environment as another person who would not feel stressed by them. This is because of the constrained system I referred to earlier. It also explained why you could not just remove the stressors and everything would be fine again.

18. Alleviating stress

Now that I understand more about people as habit machines, it's clear that scanning the external world for the causes of stress is futile. Nowadays few work situations are, in themselves, excessively stressful. We no longer slave away in noisy, grimy workhouses for sixteen hours a day or send boys up chimneys. Yes, there are frantically busy jobs, unfathomable procedures and pig-headed managers. But even these are not the general norm and they cannot account for the millions of people who claim they are 'stressed' by work. Stress comes primarily from inside the person and not from the outside world. Even supermarket checkout workers (ostensibly all doing the same job) perceive their work and the nature of its demands as vastly different – as my research has clearly demonstrated. The differences between people and how they respond to their world are much greater than the differences between jobs (especially when people do basically the same job).

This also implies something far more critical for us as people. If you want to help people under stress, changing factors in their outside world will make only a small difference at best. In fact a seismic shift in their environment would be needed to bring about even a fraction of change in the person; a shift that is probably beyond the realms of even the most visionary organisation with unlimited resources. The levers for change are in the individual, in how habitual their thinking and behaviour is. By bringing about a small change in their flexibility it will be possible to effect a large impact on the stress they experience.

So people 'create' stress. Their inflexible habits render them unable to adapt to the full range of demands that life places upon them. Their habits of the past are misaligned with their needs for the present. When they come up against a task that requires something other than their usual 'hammer' they are flummoxed, unable to cope. As a result they feel stressed. And they attribute it to the task or to another person rather than to their own limited toolset. The solution to this lies in changing the tools the person has at their disposal. It involves **flex**ing their 'personality' so they use it all, and know when and how to do so. This is much easier and more effective than trying to alter the environment in which they live and work. I have spent many years researching how this can be done. And I believe I have come up with the answers.

flex in action –
the habit-rater

Understanding your habits

With the habit-rater tool we measure your tendency to be habitual in your thinking and behaviours. We consider some common habitual tendencies, although it may well be that you have a set of habits that is particular to you too. Your score on our habit-rater may well be predictive of all manner of habits.

The habit-rater

	Please be honest. How often do you:	Always	Usually	Sometimes	Never
1	do something you said you'd give up?				
2	try something you're not very good at?				
3	say that life is boring?				
4	sit in the same spot to watch TV or eat a meal?				
5	find out about something you don't know?				
6	wear the same outfit because it's easy or comfortable?				
7	change your mind about a belief you hold?				
8	vary where you go at lunchtimes?				
9	have the same daily meals?				
10	add new people to your friendship group?				
11	express the same view?				
12	suggest ways to make work life more interesting?				
13	visit the same holiday destination?				
14	try a food or drink you think you may not like?				
15	socialise with people from different ethnic groups?				
16	visit the same shops for regular purchases?				
17	do something that others wouldn't expect of you?				
18	recall negative things that people have said or done to you?				
19	stand out from the crowd?				
20	watch a regularly scheduled TV programme?				
21	seek the opinions of different people?				
22	try to stick to a routine?				
23	get bothered when people change plans at the last minute?				
24	choose to listen to a different kind of music?				

Scoring your habit-rater

Now go to the Appendix on p170 and add up the numbers in each box that correspond to your answers. Your score should be between 0 and 72.

Interpreting your habit-rater score

Low scores (0–16)

Your score reveals you can be open-minded and flexible in the way you think and live your life. You are telling us that you are not habitual, and that you are open to new experiences and different ways of looking at things. You're also telling us you're the sort of person who's not afraid to buck the trend and go against the flow, so you have a lot to offer. You can see the value in many different types of people, not just those who are like you. Your score suggests you are flexible in what you do, the people you mix with and your interests. In your personal life your open-mindedness means you have the potential for an active and varied social life.

Flexible people are the ones who aren't frightened of challenge; they welcome and invite fresh approaches. At work this might mean, for example, they have a varied and diverse group they mix with, and even that they stir things up a bit, rather than doing what they have always done in the same way. Being less habitual makes you more responsive to the needs of your partner, your friends, your colleagues and your clients at work. You'll also be ready to embrace alternative and better ways of tackling situations and recognise that even people who don't think like you have a lot to offer. You recognise the value of doing something different.

A positive impact of the flexible and open-minded approach should be the ability to take an objective view of a situation, e.g. when issues come up, when you have decisions to take, and when you need to talk issues over. In your evaluations you are more likely to assess issues fairly against objective criteria without bias creeping in. You probably resist becoming too routinised; although habits and routines help us to manage the basics of life they can also mask opportunities that lie just beyond the range of our immediate view. Being behaviourally flexible can get around this tendency. A person who is less habitual is more likely to be open-minded and able to let go of something that's no longer working or appropriate, even if time and energy have been invested. Less habitual people are more likely to find their personal life and work more interesting and life full of opportunities for development and growth.

Medium scores (17–34)

Your score reveals that you can be less bound by habit and be open-minded and people probably see you as being pretty flexible and with a lot to offer. However, you do seem to have a slight tendency to do things the way you're used to doing them when alternative ways could be better. You might also be the type of person who could get swept along with the crowd because you don't like to rock the boat. Others might perceive you as a predictable type. The upside of this is that you're probably dependable and can be relied upon. On the other hand perhaps you're not the one they go to when looking for some 'outside the box' thinking?

Since your score suggests you have a tendency to stick to what you know and the people you know, at work or in your home life you may over-rely on approaches that have worked well for you in the past. Perhaps you even have firm views on the value of these. Could you benefit from actively inviting more challenge and fresh approaches sometimes? Even if what you currently do is successful and produces effective results, there are many advantages to be had from introducing diversity and trying fresh approaches. You might want to rethink, for example, why you mix only with the people you do, or the people you engage with at work. Are they as varied as they could be? Do you gravitate towards people you know, those who are like others you know and mix with, rather than those with another perspective or from a different background? People who don't think like you may have a lot to offer in terms of disparate perspectives and novel insights about life and making the most of it. If you open yourself up and allow them to challenge those old assumptions you could get a richer experience. Are you missing out on good relationships and input simply because some people are below your 'radar'? Being behaviourally flexible can get around this tendency.

Being less habitual in how you respond to others might also make you more responsive to the needs of your partner, your friends, your colleagues and your clients at work. Might it also make things more interesting and effective? Perhaps a less habitual set of behaviours might help you get more of what you want out of life.

Your score indicates you may sometimes find it helpful to take a more objective view of a situation. This might be when issues come up with your partner, friends or colleagues, when you have decisions to take, and when you need to talk issues over with others. Do you have a tendency to think what you think without sufficient reflection on the issues? Or do you try hard to ensure you don't compare against what you know or are familiar with?

Be wary of becoming too routinised; although habits and routines help us to manage the basics of life they can also mask opportunities that lie just beyond the range of our immediate view. Could you benefit from doing something different? Also, people who are too routinised may be reluctant to let go of something that's no longer working or appropriate. Perhaps a tendency to keep investing time and energy in long-standing client relationships that no longer warrant it, when it might be better to keep it ticking over and move on?

If you sometimes find life difficult or uninteresting, stressful and lacking opportunities for development and growth, becoming less habitual and developing your open-mindedness could make a difference.

High scores (35+)
Your score reveals that you view yourself as having a good stock of tried and tested ways of doing things. This can be a good thing; you have a lot to offer and others will probably see you as solid and dependable. However, at times you might profit from being more open-minded and less routinised. Adding a variety of experiences to your life could widen your horizons, expand the scope of opportunities that come your way and even make life a little easier for you. Looking at things from a different perspective and trying new approaches to what you do may help you get more from life and relationships. When we adhere too rigidly to routines and strongly held views we risk closing off all sorts of positive avenues.

Your score suggests you prefer to stick to what you know and the people you know. That's a natural tendency that many of us have. In your home and/or work life you may have decided which approaches are best and even have firm views on these. This is fine, but sometimes it's also beneficial for everyone to invite challenge and welcome fresh approaches. You may think that the way you do things is successful and produces effective results. You may, of course, be right. But there may be advantages to be had from sometimes breaking free of the usual ways of doing things and giving new approaches a try.

You might want to rethink, for example, how you deal with issues that come up with your partner, your friends or your colleagues. Do you address new issues with old thinking? Do you make assumptions because of your past thoughts and experiences? When you have decisions to take, or when you need to talk issues over with others, do you know what you are going to say and think in advance? Do you have a tendency to think what you think without sufficient reflection on the issues? Or without sufficient consideration of the other people involved? Do you allow others to challenge those old assumptions now and again? That might provide you with a richer experience or a new solution, or a new way of thinking.

Do your friends and acquaintances have the same values, interests and ways of looking at things? How similar are they in background and views? Do you have a one-size-fits-all approach? Are you missing out on good relationships, good friends and valuable input simply because some people aren't picked up on your 'radar'? Can you be responsive to life's needs and those of your family and friends if your decisions are hampered by stereotyped assumptions? Less habitual thinking brings with it a greater ability to take an objective view of a situation.

Although it can be useful to have habits and routines – after all, they help us to manage the basics of life – they can also mask opportunities that lie just beyond the range of our immediate view. Being behaviourally flexible can get around this tendency.

A drawback to being too routinised can be a reluctance to let go of something that's no longer working or appropriate. There may be a tendency to keep investing time and energy in long-standing relationships that no longer warrant it, when it might be better to simply keep them ticking over or even move on.

If you sometimes find life or work uninteresting, stressful and lacking opportunities for development and growth perhaps you could benefit from **flex** and from doing something different?

flex yourself – Do Something Different

The easiest way to break old habits is to try new behaviours. Using willpower won't work but substituting new behaviours for old ones will.

And when you're doing something you don't normally do, it goes without saying that you can't stick to your old ways. This is when the law of unintended consequences starts to work. You may not *know* what's going to happen when you break a habit. But if you can be *open* to new experiences and new opportunities, who knows what will come your way?

If you hang on to your old habits and your old ways it's likely that life will just stay the same. And if there are bits of that life you're not happy with, there's a danger that the present will become permanent. So, as your first venture into opening up the other 9/10ths of your personality, why not just try a few simple things from the following list … and see what happens:

- Leave your watch off for a day.
- Make the first move to repair a broken friendship.
- Go for a walk and take photos of what you see.
- Pick up some litter or rubbish.
- Watch birds or clouds for ten minutes.
- Sit in a place you've never sat before.
- Make up a quiz.
- Come up with three good conversation-starter questions.
- Sing with your granny.
- Tell a joke to a stranger.
- Spend time with someone much older.
- Ask advice from someone much younger.
- Tell a friend why you like them.
- Smile at people more.
- Do something nice for an older person.

- Buy an unusual magazine and read it.
- Change radio channels or start listening to one.
- Let another person choose from the menu for you.
- Get on a bus and see where it takes you.
- Wear odd socks for a day.
- Communicate by painting or drawing.
- Contact a long lost friend or relation.
- Write an impressive CV.
- Learn about a ritual from another religion.
- Read a different newspaper.
- Dance under the stars.
- Play louder music.
- Give a gift, without expecting to receive anything.
- Get a temporary tattoo and wear it somewhere visible.
- Repair or renew something that's broken.
- Sleep on the other side (or end) of the bed.
- Pick CDs at random and play track 8.
- Do something you enjoyed doing as a child.
- Go barefoot.
- Turn up at the cinema and watch the next film that's starting.
- Open a book at random and read for half an hour.
- Start volunteering.

We have run many DSD programmes and interventions (some of which we'll talk more about later) and one of the people who took part told us she had got the DSD 'bug'. That's because new experiences bring about pleasurable feelings that are self-reinforcing. So staying with a DSD programme isn't an effort; it's something that people want to do because of the returns it brings and it usually becomes a way of life. A big mindset shift that people doing DSD undergo is the realisation that waiting for the world to change is futile.

It won't. And trying to change the world is also a tough task. But changing the way you experience the world, simply by doing something different, is something that everyone can manage. And, as another person who tried DSD told us:

'When you do something different something magical happens.'

More of that later, but for now let's go on to look at why it's such a powerful way to change.

2

Section 2:
Behavioural flexibility

19. The birth of FIT Science

I developed a new branch of psychology, known as FIT Science, which focuses on personal development and the qualities that determine success and well-being. It wasn't enough to say that person-based factors play a key role in stress, performance, relationships and decision-making. Or simply to blame people's habits. We needed a model that explained what a person could change in order to cope better with their existence and lead a fuller life. There was a need to identify which behavioural dimensions a broad personality should encompass. And to know which underlying traits would keep them flexible. These led me to develop and test a new model.

I called my new model FIT Science: FIT stands for 'Framework for Internal Transformation'. I developed FIT Science when I was dean of a large business school (at the University of Hertfordshire) and had been working on these ideas for some years.

As a consequence of my stress research I had already produced the Work FIT Profiler (then called the Micro-Cultural Audit) – a tool that measured work demands, supports and constraints and a plethora of important outcomes (stress, performance, commitment and teamwork, amongst other things.). One of my PhD students, Bob Stead, was researching the effects of long hours of work on well-being. We came up with the idea of measuring the key factors that are at the root of how people perform, what makes them see things the way they do, both in their work and in life generally.

Some years earlier I had published some groundbreaking research looking at occupational mortality in a new way. Essentially, my research demonstrated that the life expectancy – and precise cause of death of a married woman – could be predicted from her husband's job. This was true for all causes of death, even suicide, accidents, different cancers, multiple sclerosis and so on. I showed that there were very subtle but powerful psychological processes at work in determining mortality, both occupational and disease-specific across the 500-plus jobs I analysed. For example, police sergeants (and their wives) had high cancer mortality, builders' labourers (and their wives) high accident mortality and musicians (and their wives) high respiratory disease mortality. The effects were not owing to social class differences. There were many factors that could be responsible for such findings but – with the help of another PhD student, Fiona Jones – I came to the conclusion that these predictable deaths were owing to changes in what I called 'cognitive architecture' brought about by marriage and the shared psychological environment, or the common ways in which couples come to perceive and interact with their world. That architecture became FIT.

With Bob Stead, I set about ways of defining and measuring that architecture, which resulted in the FIT Profiler. We tested many hundreds of people with early versions of the Profiler and looked at all factors in relation to FIT. FIT Science, and the measuring tools necessary to study it, now existed explicitly. In 2000 we published *(Inner) FITness and The FIT Corporation* (Thompson International Press).

FIT Science is a way of profiling the breadth of a person's personality. It measures an individual's five key elements of thinking, which we called the 'constancies' because they are always important in what we think and do, and fifteen different aspects of behaviour, known as 'behavioural dimensions'. A FIT person has both 'inner' and 'outer' FITness:

- Inner FITness is when decisions are made on the basis of the five FIT 'constancies' or thinking dimensions. These are described below.
- Outer FITness is when the person has the broadest possible behavioural repertoire. In a sense, a 'whole' personality. In the original model this behavioural flexibility was made up of fifteen behavioural dimensions. Outer FITness is the external or observable 'personality' of the individual.

According to FIT Science, the combination of these 'inner' and 'outer' FIT elements determines how a person sees him or herself and can measure the full extent of their behavioural repertoire. They also account for all decision-making and how well a person copes with life and gets along with others. They are key in terms of performance and getting on and not letting habits run your life.

A person can be FIT to a greater or lesser degree in terms of both their inner and outer FITness. Inner and outer FITness are independent of each other, so that a person can appear to optimise their observable behaviours but be weak on the inside, or they can be strong on the inside but this does not manifest in their behaviour because they are not flexible enough.

20. Inner FITness – constancies

The FIT constancies are, in essence, the core building blocks of how we perceive and act in the world. Together these five constancies determine a person's inner FITness, or their cognitive architecture. They are:

- awareness
- fearlessness
- self-responsibility
- conscience and
- balance.

The constancies are the core qualities a person needs to develop in order to overcome the pull of habits and expand their personality.

21. Awareness

This is the degree to which an individual monitors and attends to their internal and external world, the degree to which they can be said to be awake to all relevant aspects of themselves and any given situation.

Awareness is the opposite of habits and doing things on autopilot. Awareness includes attending to thoughts and sensory information in the moment. A central aspect of awareness is attention to 'relevant' detail. We all become habituated to look at the world through old eyes and see and sense what we have seen and sensed before. But there is much more available for our senses to see than what our automatic pilot points us towards. Consider all the sensory information from the environment around you now. Interrogate how you are sitting, precisely what made you read this, how aware you have been over the last thirty seconds, the degree to which you were aware of the factors at work in the last interaction you had with someone, and so on.

Awareness includes having insight into your own motives and needs, as well as the likely motives and needs of others. It also includes self-awareness in the broadest sense. It includes an awareness of options. It includes an awareness of when we are being driven by habit too, and whether that is good or bad for us at the time.

We now know that most of the time we are not very aware. I would guess we are aware less than 1 per cent of the time about less than 1 per cent of the possibilities. That is normal. But a FIT person has sufficient awareness to turn off the autopilot when needed and when appropriate, in order to make the most of situations and opportunities.

22. Fearlessness

This is acting without fear or trepidation, or essentially facing the unknown with the same bravado as the known.

Doing things without fear is necessary, not only for our emotional well-being, but also to help us do the right things. If we are fearful about future situations we will avoid them. Habit drives us towards the safe, the known and the comfortable. Yet fear is a major problem that inhibits so much of what people do. It affects us all at times. In my view, fear has no role to play in shaping decisions and behaviour in the modern world, although I am aware that many people disagree with this. When giving talks on FIT Science over the years I have been challenged on this many times. Of course, I appreciate that fear has a primal function. It protects animals from dangers, but that is in the jungle, in the past, or in a completely different context. We do not live in the jungle or in the past anymore and these basic animal instincts have little relevance to modern life. I would even question the benefit – for a cognate human being – of fear in any situation. Sure, if I am on the edge of a big drop I will be fearful but I don't think that fear is protective there either – speaking for myself only, I think the fear would be more likely to make me fall! It might even make some jump.

Being fearless is not just about doing things without the feeling of fear surfacing in your thoughts. In some situations it is actually better to feel the fear and do the right thing. I am reminded of one person whose FIT Profiler clearly showed him to be low on the fearless constancy, meaning that he was quite fearful. Over time he was profiled several times and always disagreed with this profile as he thought that fear did not drive his decisions and actions. The penny dropped one day when he realised this was because he made sure he never did those things that might cause him to feel fearful. He had constructed his life in such a way that it kept him safe from any risk of feeling this emotion. It had worked so far, but he had shrunk his world and that was one reason he was really being held back.

This case also illustrates another important point about fearlessness. It is necessary to unearth the fears that are masked by the habitual behaviours and natural tendencies we all have. I believe that by being hidden these fears can do us more damage than if we faced and overcame them. The family of fear (including phobia, anxieties, nervousness and trepidation, for example) influences many behaviours and decisions that people make, although it may not be apparent. Fear can have a strong grip on our unconscious actions and often does not allow our conscious thoughts into this secret. So we need to be aware of the hidden traps and later we'll see how Do Something Different helps to expose them.

23. Self-responsibility

This is the degree to which an individual accepts personal accountability for their world irrespective of the impact of factors outside themselves.

People get what they take responsibility for. That is true of you and me. It is true for all of us. If ten different people are put in the same situation, what each makes of it will be more determined by their levels of self-responsibility than by their talents and skills. I have witnessed many examples of high levels of self-responsibility overcoming enormous practical and societal barriers. In business, for example, a high degree of self-responsibility can make up for a lack of educational advantage. People who refuse to blame others for problems and issues gain the resources and experience to overcome them themselves. Yet it seems to me – when I listen to others talk in most situations – that people think the world 'out there' determines what happens to them. 'They' – those faceless others who seem so central to the lives of people – seem to be perceived to be the primary shapers.

There are many 'they's for all of us: the government, our bosses, the media, society. But the hand that life apparently deals us is the way it is *because* we think and act as if 'they' control things, not because they do. There are all sorts of reasons why people feel they cannot take self-responsibility (genetics, upbringing, lack of resources or help from others) but to maximise the opportunity in any situation it's essential to be self-responsible and not leave the outcome to others or to chance.

In essence, the self-responsibility constancy is about removing the psychological constraints we all put on our options and actions. It is more about trying to live as if we are 'God in our own universe'. Because in the end the world is a reflection of yourself. What opportunities are missed because we like the comfort zone of dependence? Because we like not exercising the freedom and control we have. We like chaining ourselves to an outside world. We like not being responsible. It does not have to be like this.

Don't wait for catastrophe to force changes on you.

It is sad when people suffer some major life event or catastrophe, perhaps a major illness, a partner leaving, an accident, the unexpected death of someone dear. As a consequence, though, some people are released from the vice-like grip of their habitual ways of behaving. The catastrophe can bring about new beginnings. The person may be freed up to do things they had previously wanted to do – perhaps give up a job, travel somewhere, make a big change in their daily life. It is a pity – and unnecessary – to wait for a major catastrophe. Why not take the liberty and make the moves or improve things now, whilst you are still in the driving seat?

A word about luck

The word 'luck' crops up all the time in conversations and in people's attributions of success and failure. It seems knitted into the fabric of many people's lives. I think luck will fill the vacuum if self-responsibility is not exercised. So, the degree to which you believe in luck may be a good (inverse) barometer of your own level of self-responsibility. Our lives will inevitably be shaped by many forces such as the demands of others, genetics and finances, but the absence of inner direction and choice makes it certain that 'luck' will reign. Research makes it clear that being lucky is not a happenchance – we make our own luck by our behaviours, by our efforts and by our own beliefs and actions. Random factors, synchronicity, astrological charts and supernatural forces can operate only in a world where choices are not shaped and taken by individuals. If you want to predict the future you have to shape it yourself.

24. Balance

Making sure each aspect of life receives due care and attention. For any aspect of life, there needs to be equivalence between the level of importance we assign to it, the level of effort we put into it, and the satisfaction resulting from it.

The balance constancy judges value and worth. Balance has two different aspects:

1. The balance between *importance, satisfaction and effort.*
   I call this *levels balance.*

2. The balance between *different areas of life.* I call this *life balance.*

In terms of levels balance, this is achieved when the importance level, satisfaction level and effort level are equivalent. The levels in each measure might be high or low, but they need to be the same. Imbalance occurs, for example, if you think that something is important (e.g. a particular relationship, an activity you do, or a value you hold), but it does not make you very happy or you do not put the appropriate level of effort into it. The imbalance can be the result of either too much or too little of the three factors – importance, satisfaction and effort.

In terms of life balance, past research in FIT Science has concentrated on three life elements:

- work or job
- non-work or domestic, social and interpersonal activities and
- self.

The key here is to have life in balance across all three areas. A great deal of attention in the media and in academic research has been placed on work–life balance. This focus on work–life balance fails to account for the centrality of the self. Aspects of self include how individuals view themselves in terms of value in the context of what they do. It includes such things as self-efficacy (the belief that you can be effective in the world), self-developmental aspects and general self-worth. It is not uncommon for people to put themselves last when making work or non-work decisions. Mothers, for example, may engage in self-sacrifice for the benefit of their children. By contrast, others put themselves before all other considerations in their decisions and actions. Some people believe this to be true of bankers, prior to the economic collapse in 2008. Balance involves getting the effort–importance–satisfaction equation right for all three areas. Balance is achieved by ensuring that no one area is dominant.

25. Conscience

Differentiating right from wrong and doing what is right.

Conscience sets the limits for our behaviours and the decisions that we make. Conscience is about bringing the moral and ethical dimensions to bear in our decisions and behaviours and helping us to do the right thing. Not acting habitually or automatically.

Embedded moral and ethical matters

One question I have been frequently asked is, 'Who am I to say what is right and wrong?' That misses the main point. It is important to consider the moral and ethical dimensions in what we do, and to consider where moral and ethical matters are relevant. People often make decisions, or behave in a particular way, without even thinking there might be a moral or ethical aspect to the situation. Forgetting to consider the moral or ethical dimension of situations is probably responsible for more immoral actions than deliberately choosing to be immoral. For example, careless littering, an unconsidered remark, failure to recycle garbage, acting without thinking out of habit, or without due care and attention may be responsible for unethical or immoral outcomes. Often these actions would have been different had the perpetrator thought about matters more. These are different from the more conscious immoral actions, such as having unprotected sex with someone when knowingly infected with HIV, but they do have consequences nonetheless.

In FIT Science, the moral and ethical is always the right choice. There are no ifs or buts. There are no compromises for personal advantage, or hedonism, or for a good time.

However, what is moral and ethical may be determined by the situation or context. So the individual has to consider the situation from the view of being totally self-responsible, fearless, balanced and aware. By so doing they will be able to consider the consequences, in moral and ethical terms, of their actions.

The importance of conscience – other than in the moral and ethical context – can also be seen clearly when we consider the short-term and long-term consequences of our actions. Some people may well consider it to be OK to behave in a certain way in the short term, but not when the consequences unravel over time. People often come unstuck for not taking account of the longer game. For example, people often say that small misdemeanours that others don't notice at the time do no harm. Even if this were true (it is often just an excuse), such behaviours can cause problems later on. Perhaps the person forgets what they said? Keeping a web of lies supported can tax even the best memory. Perhaps the small moral crack opens up a larger chasm with gradual moral decline. FIT Science takes the broader, longer-term perspective as the backdrop against which to consider one's conscience in decisions and behaviours.

26. Harmony among the constancies

In the FIT framework, the target for personal development and growth is to achieve higher levels of the constancies. In *(Inner) FITness* I outlined five different levels of development – from the lowest, Level 1 or 'dependent' stage, in which the individual is shaped by external forces, through to the 'charismatic' level, when the person is in full control of themselves and any outcomes.

Personal development requires developing each of the constancies to their maximal extent. No one I know has demonstrated the highest level of development to become 'God in their own universe', but I have seen people's FIT Profilers measuring as low as 10 per cent on each constancy up to the 90 per cents. Being low on a constancy is likely to bring with it certain negative consequences. The table below shows some examples:

Being too low in ...	... may lead to:
Awareness	Insensitivity Lost opportunities Poor relationships
Fearlessness	Anxiety and illness Playing too safe Disappointment
Self-responsibility	Perceiving no control Being impressionable Lack of direction
Balance	Failure Over-focus Chasing one's tail
Conscience	Damage to others Long-term costs Prejudice

From the thousands of people who have been FIT profiled, we have seen some who score relatively high in one constancy compared to the others. This lack of 'harmony' can itself cause problems because personal outcomes are dependent on all five constancies and each acts as a check and balance on decisions and actions. The table below shows some of the more common problems of having high levels of a constancy not balanced by other constancies:

Being too high in ...	... can result in:
Awareness	Hypersensitivity Self-absorption Hypochondria
Fearlessness	Reckless actions Danger Self-harm
Self-responsibility	Obstinacy Dogmatism Bullying
Balance	Mediocrity Decision paralysis Missed opportunities
Conscience	Preaching, not practising Intolerance of others Nit-picking

Some people are so fearless that they do reckless things that cause harm to themselves and others. Some people are so aware that they cannot cross the street for fear of being run over. Some people are so self-responsible that they fail to get others to do what they should do and end up stressed out. Some people are so concerned about doing the right thing that other people get fed up being told what they are doing wrong. Some people balance things in their life but have no passion. The 'good' inner FIT ingredients may have negative consequences for a person unless he or she can achieve harmony among the constancies.

So, am I saying that people should become less FIT in these areas for their own good? No. The solution lies in bringing harmony to all the constancies, so that they hold each other in check. The best way to do this is to work on raising the weaker levels, rather than reducing the higher ones. Fearlessness does need to be held at bay, as do all the constancies, but they do that for each other. That is why achieving harmony among the constancy levels – where each one is as strong as the others – is an important target to aim for.

27. Outer FITness – behavioural flexibility

We have so far described the dimensions of FIT Science that are concerned with thinking or cognition – the inner part of FITness. These constancies are fundamental to effectiveness and well-being in the broadest sense. All our research shows us that. But these constancies are not where the action is. It is very difficult for us to simply change our minds and be less fearful, or more self-responsible.

We cannot *think* ourselves better and the plethora of failed self-help books illustrates this. Positive thinking is a great idea but often so difficult to put into practice, particularly if we have got into the habit of thinking otherwise. We cannot just be told to be different, or even tell ourselves. For the vast majority of people willpower (if it exists) is just not strong enough to battle against a lifetime of habits. We have to do something different to make change possible.

That is where the outer part of FITness comes in. It sets the base from which we can start to change for the better. Our behaviours shape our thoughts. What we do can be used to bring about change. If we behave differently we start to think differently as a consequence of the new experiences we have. So behaviours can change constancies; behaviours can change minds.

In FIT Science we start with the behaviours that we naturally have in our repertoire. These are our own personal habit map; they are our 'personality'. As I told the Chinese waiter, the difficulty with describing behaviour in terms of personality traits (such as the 'big five': agreeableness, conscientiousness, extroversion, neuroticism and openness to experience), however, is that it suggests an inherent inflexibility. Your personality habit travels everywhere with you and whatever the real needs of the situation, or whatever would be best for you, you do as you have generally done before probably using only 1/10th of your potential 'personality'. That is habitual and inflexible behaviour. It is basic behaviour without thought for need. It is running on automatic pilot. As we saw earlier, this doesn't allow a person to grow and can even cause them to struggle with life. In fact our ingrained reactions and automatic behaviours:

- often have bad consequences for us and/or those around us
- may not be relevant to the present demands of the situation
- are owing to our genes and our upbringing, or are modelled on other people, and may not best serve us as adults
- impact negatively on how we feel
- impact negatively on others and how we are perceived and
- are often at odds with how we *think* we are behaving because in the main habits bypass conscious processing.

So, there is a sound rationale for *not* acting habitually or doing 'what comes naturally'. I am filled with trepidation when I hear people advising others to 'just be yourself'. The chances are, that is the one thing *not* to be. Doing what comes naturally can be good but it has a risk of doing damage because a given trait will be inappropriate in more situations than it can be appropriate for. Our personality habits are often a poor match for the very varied world in which we live.

That is why it is better to be behaviourally flexible: FIT Science has this notion at its core. That is why it is sometimes better to do what doesn't come naturally! To make the most of ourselves we need to **flex** ourselves and go against our natural tendencies.

28. Behavioural dimensions

The FIT Profiler measures fifteen different 'behavioural dimensions'. Since the original FIT Profiler was developed, thousands of people have completed Profilers and provided their data to help me refine my ideas about what the important behavioural dimensions are. This has also shown how reliable the tool has been over the years. The key behavioural dimensions are shown in the table below:

Key behavioural dimensions	
Unassertive	Assertive
Trusting	Wary
Calm/relaxed	Energetic/driven
Reactive	Proactive
Definite	Flexible[1]
Risk-taker	Plays safe
Behave as others want	Behave as you wish
Spontaneous	Systematic
Single-minded	Open-minded
Introverted	Extroverted
Conventional	Unconventional
Individually-centred	Group-centred
Firm	Gentle
Lively	Laid back
Predictable	Unpredictable

The original FIT Profiler has been subjected to full psychometric analysis and is highly reliable.[2] In general, people do not come out very flexible, as I had expected. Across all fifteen dimensions the average score people get for their behavioural flexibility suggests they use about 22 per cent of their potential behaviours. Some use as little as 10 per cent and about one in five people show no flexibility whatsoever – they appear to have firmly entrenched personalities. People who are using as much as 50 per cent of their possible behaviour repertoire are very rare indeed.

At the end of this section you can find out how to **flex** yourself further along these dimensions.

---

1. 'Flexible' here refers to being changeable and adaptable. flex is about being able to use an appropriate behavioural response to a situation. Some situations might require the person to flex by being definite, meaning that being flexible is only right when it's appropriate to the situation.

2. The behavioural flexibility scale, for example, has a Cronbach's alpha of 0.914 (the maximum score is 1, and this would be considered to show very strong reliability). The scale is also statistically sound in that it has a single large factor that underlies it, without any indications to suggest that the measure has other components.

29. Doing the right thing

Being flexible doesn't necessarily guarantee you'll do the right thing in a situation. It is crucial not only to have as wide a repertoire of acceptable behaviours as possible, but also to deploy them appropriately as the situation demands. Flexible behaviour is no good if you always seem to pull out an inappropriate behaviour!

It is the constancies that ensure that behaviour is optimal. In reality, however, people do not score perfect 100 per cent scores on the five constancies (called 'FIT integrity'). Also, that many people's profiles show a considerable lack of harmony among the constancies creates additional problems for doing the right thing.

Our behavioural habits, however, create the biggest obstacle. We just don't notice how our personality traits keep us behaviourally cooped up. Our 'comfort zone' is somewhere we (and our brains) like us to be. Staying in the comfort zone is also a self-defence mechanism for dealing with uncertainly and stress – we cut out the world by behaving as if some parts of it are not present. We want the uncertainty to disappear. So we even categorise the new as the old, for example, when having been seasick on a rough ferry crossing makes someone turn down their next chance to visit somewhere potentially exciting. Many people prefer the certain and the known (i.e. they know they won't get seasick on dry land so never go farther afield). And our personality – our narrow range of behaviours – suits us well. It fits what we see and do, because we reshape our world to fit, not because we try harder to fit with the world.

This is why we need to do something different and really new to help increase our behavioural flexibility. Otherwise the pull of the comfort zone is too strong and habits spring back to guide how we respond. In our experience, people often need a 'licence' to move outside their habits, and when they do, things turn out to be fun and interesting, and not as 'uncomfortable' as they had feared.

30. The stress and inefficiency zone

To illustrate the problems that are caused by habitual behaviours and the comfort zones, look at Figure 1. It illustrates one person's comfort zone on just one behavioural dimension, unassertiveness–assertiveness. Each end of the dimensional scale has a darker shaded area. These signify the unacceptable ends of the dimension. So being extremely assertive might be bullying or even killing others. Extreme unassertiveness might manifest as being very inert or even comatose. The paler shaded area in between, making up most of the bar, represents a possible range of acceptable behaviours that could be used according to circumstance. All of those behaviours would be acceptable, but whether they are ideal would depend upon the particular circumstance or situation.

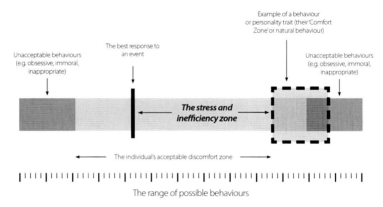

1. flex and personality traits

The box represents the constrained personality of one individual. In this case theirs includes some unacceptable behaviours (the box overlaps the darker end of the scale so, for example, perhaps the person is sometimes violent with their partner).

The range of behaviours they feel comfortable using (illustrated by the box) is very small. They're probably using only 1/10th of their potential repertoire. This could be because they are habitual, inflexible or lacking in awareness of how they come across.

As the person is at the assertive end of the scale, a large range of acceptable behaviours fall *outside* their comfort zone. When a situation occurs that requires a behaviour not in their range (represented by the vertical line on the diagram) the consequences for them will usually be negative. It may be, for example, that they know they should be doing things differently but cannot – perhaps out of habit or ignorance of what the right action would be. In this situation they are likely to experience a good deal of stress. We call the gap between their personality range and the situational demand the 'stress and inefficiency zone'.

This person has a narrow range of personality-led behaviours and may not even realise there are other ways of responding. This may not lead to stress in the short term in them (because they are unaware), but it is likely to be a very unproductive and ineffective way of getting the most out of life. It will probably cause stress and negative feelings in others too, and the 'kick-back' from others may cause further stress in the longer term.

31. Behaving differently with different people

Of course, many people do behave differently with different people. Some people do not stay in the same personality box all the time. Figure 2, for example, shows the same person we saw above but this time interacting with a work colleague (person 2) rather than with their spouse (person 1). The range of behaviour the person displays shows a very different pattern.

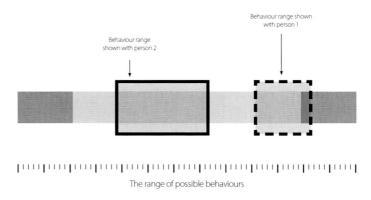

2. Person-specific comfort zones and behaviour

In the figure the person shows a wider range of acceptable behaviours towards their work colleague (person 2) than towards their spouse (person 1). Here none of the behaviours towards their colleague are in the unacceptable zone. They also appear to be able to **flex** much more – to show a much broader range of behaviour – towards their colleague than towards their spouse. For example, they can be both assertive and unassertive at work. This does not imply that they are behaving any more appropriately with their work colleague, however, since the ideal is to behave according to the particular demands of the situation. It may be that they are more unassertive with person 2 but would generally benefit from being more assertive with them. This brings out two key aspects to do with behavioural flexibility. To **flex** properly we need to take account of:

- the who, and
- the why.

The person who is the target of our behaviour, as well as the context or conditions for the behaviour, are important for **flex**. If we cannot take adequate account of both these aspects, it is likely that we are allowing our habits and our automatic pilot to determine what happens. We may even be ignoring 9/10ths of our 'personality'. This may be OK sometimes, but more often than not will be less effective for us, them, and the outcomes of what we do. Good intentions are good, but never as good as actually doing the right thing in the right situation to the right person.

32. The optimal behavioural range

Figure 3 below shows the perfect range of behaviour that ideally a person should aim for.

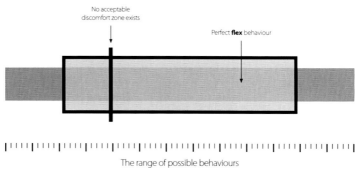

The range of possible behaviours

3. Being able to cope with anything

Having the broad spectrum of behaviours shown above, on all the fifteen dimensions of behaviour, would demonstrate ultimate **flex.** Not just 1/10th of the potential behaviours are at the person's disposal but the full complement, the full '10/10ths'. And there is absolutely no reason why in principle everyone could not achieve this. After all we all have the potential to develop behaviours and responses that we don't naturally have. In practice I have not seen anybody score near 100 (the maximum possible) for behaviour flexibility on the FIT Profiler. People do often show that they have behaviours on both sides of some of the behavioural dimensions (so they report being both extrovert and introvert, for example), even though they may not completely **flex** across the entire range, or on all of the fifteen dimensions.

33. Making the most of a situation includes you too

In an ideal world, if you want to get the most from a situation, it would be the situational demands – and not your natural tendencies or habits – that would determine your response and behaviour. Precisely which behaviour is needed from you will not be just a matter of those situational demands, however, because what is right for you also has to be taken into account. The role of the five constancies in FIT Science is to guide you to do what is right for you.

Coherence is important too.

Maximising the situational opportunities means including yourself in the equation too. Being 100 per cent fearless, 100 per cent self-responsible, 100 per cent in balance, 100 per cent backed by conscience and 100 per cent aware (i.e. having 100 per cent FIT integrity) may not guarantee that the behaviour is right for you. This is because, as humans, we also have drives, desires, motivations, thoughts, intentions, reflections and memories. We live in a social world and we communicate with each other and have a social context to take account of too. FIT integrity and the constancies cannot take account of all these aspects of the self. We need to be *coherent* (in ourselves and in the social world), as well as making the most of our world – something we will return to in the next section of the book.

34. flex transition – relabelling feelings and repetition

Knowing what the right thing is for you in a given situation and doing it, however, are quite different things. People find the pull of natural and habitual behaviours very strong indeed. One reason for this is the feeling of discomfort people get when they try behaviours they are not used to. Going outside the comfort zone of one's habitual personality takes conscious effort to begin with. As does coping with the feelings that accompany a trip into the 'discomfort zone' such as when we do something different.

When we get people to do something different in our programmes some say they find that even trivial changes feel strange. Not watching the TV for one evening, for example, leaves people wondering what to do with the time. Sitting in a different seat to have dinner, a very minor step outside the norm, some say feels weird to them. Getting people to change seats during our group training sessions even meets with some resistance and questioning!

There is nothing intrinsically negative in the discomfort zone (if it involves doing the right thing) except the fact that the feelings signify you are doing something that may not come naturally.

In some ways, **flex** transition involves an exercise in relabelling those feelings. The feelings can serve as a really positive indicator that you are entering a new developmental phase. Instead of a negative label you need to learn to give them a positive label. To do this does, of course, mean that you need to prove to yourself that the new behaviours you are trying have value for you. This will be difficult if you are unable to separate the effects of the new behaviour from the initial negative attributions you give to the discomfort zone. So this may require a little experimentation, practice and repetition. There is often a 'feelings lag' when doing something new and you have to give this time to disappear. That is one reason you need to persevere when you enter the discomfort zone. It is a place of growth and if you can keep that in mind it will get easier.

35. Moving on and expanding tastes too

Let me give you an example of this that I have found repeatedly in my own life. I am a child of the 60s – a 'baby boomer' and a hippy who 'got into' rock music and all the old favourites of that era, such as The Beatles, Bob Dylan, Genesis, Led Zeppelin and the like. Good music. Many of my friends still like the music of their past. But times change. And there is so much more music easily available now. It would be narrow-minded to restrict oneself to a tiny portion of all the good music that exists in the world. The musical world expands so much when you can add a genre of music to what you love. So I decided to work by a simple rule. If music within a genre is considered 'the best' by those that love that genre I do not dismiss it because it is not to my (natural or learned) taste. I work on the assumption that it must be good; it is just that I have not learned to like it yet because it is in my discomfort zone.

So I have expanded what I think (and feel) is some outstanding music. I have sought out and tried some of the best in all kinds of genres and made a point of listening to it. Not just once or twice. If a musical expert says it is the best there is, then I take time to try to learn why it is good. And, over the years, I have come to love many types of music – not just classical and modern but also the most avant-garde and way out from all around the world. And I have totally revised my thinking about what is and isn't dull.

I think by doing this I have expanded my love of music 1000-fold. I can now appreciate and value so much more and I believe my life is richer and more expansive for having done so. I retain discrimination and taste within each genre, so repetition does not always turn out to my liking. But I am open to the notion that it is good because many find it so. I have needed to give my feelings and thoughts time to catch up with this fact.

This is an example in a small area of personal choice. But this can be applied to many areas of life where you might feel negative or discomfort towards something. People, customs, hobbies, activities, performances. Try to understand why others are excited by something outside your usual experience. Try exposing yourself to it instead of dismissing it. Avoid that habit we're all prone to of jumping to a habitual conclusion based on little evidence. Doing this may enlighten you to a whole host of new opportunities that you would previously have been closed off to.

This exploration is likely to reveal where you have deep-seated bias and prejudice in your everyday attitudes and opinions too. You might have fixed reasons for objecting to why governments or your bosses make the decisions they do. Or why your own habits mean that you get the reactions you get from others, when you were hoping for a different response. Once these are exposed you can set about being more open to the new. You may catch yourself bemoaning something unfamiliar that has appeared in your life. Perhaps your local shop has been taken over by folk from a different culture. Or another piece of technology has come out that you have resisted embracing. Instead of dismissing it, why not force yourself to try it out? Often we need to feel the discomfort of trying to act differently to see why our habitual responses have the outcomes they normally do.

The key to being open to the new and ready to learn and accept difference is to be constantly open to it. Habits, by their very nature, don't break down easily and try to steer us away from the unfamiliar and back to the comfort zone. It often takes a few exposures to the new to begin to understand how constraining and limiting our habits of thinking and behaviour have been.

Does this repeated exposure always work? Perhaps not. Are there areas of life where this approach does not work? Perhaps. But we can never know which attempts will or won't be successful until we open ourselves up with repeated tests of our own habits.

Habits can, as we have mentioned, also be very good for us. But to achieve our full potential we do need to subject them to a check every now and again. We need to regularly put ourselves into the discomfort zone so that we can question and scrutinise them and ask ourselves honestly if the habits we have continue to serve us well. Or whether they are conspiring to shrink our world even further.

36. Back to stress and the discomfort zone

If a person has a small set of possible behaviours – as in the example in Figure 1 – this is likely to mean that their corresponding stress zone is big. People with a limited range of behaviours deal with many situations in an ineffective and inefficient way because their natural behaviours are unlikely to be appropriate for making the most of a situation. A small behavioural repertoire makes for a big stress potential. That's because, as we have seen, the person will encounter many life situations they are inadequately equipped to deal with effectively. It is for this reason that behavioural flexibility is a good prophylactic for stress. In fact, expanding our behavioural repertoires can help us to minimise anxiety and depression, low self-esteem and low self-efficacy. **flex** is about making your stress or inefficiency zone as small as possible.

A common reaction to this from those with 'strong' personalities, or those with a narrow range of behaviours who happen to have been successful, is denial. When a person does behave in a way they are not used to, or when this is suggested, a common response is to deny the need to behave differently or simply to refuse to do it. Some are very insistent that their particular mix of behaviours happens to be the right one for being successful. This is illogical, of course, as well as narrowly focused. I cannot deny their success (although, as I previously noted, it is often accompanied by other life and relationship costs), but there is an undeniable logic in the idea that having a wider toolset of behaviours better equips a person to deal with a broader range of situations.

37. New behaviours have effects on others

Other people probably like you the way you are. That's how they know you, and of course they have habits too. The habits of thinking they have mean that if you behave differently they will:

- notice a difference because your new behaviour breaks an expectation they had about you and because they need to work out how to respond to the new you and

- find it a bit uncomfortable because your comfort zone of behaviours is their comfort zone too.

Friends have an investment in you staying the way you are, even if this is not in either your best interests or theirs. I remember a very good friend of mine being annoyed at me for breaking up my relationship with my partner at that time. Initially I thought his reaction was because he believed I was being unkind to her, or perhaps he thought I was making a mistake. In fact it turned out that the real reason for his annoyance was that it would cause disruption to *his* life. We would no longer be a foursome who could go on those holidays and evenings out that he found so enjoyable. Similarly, a student we know decided to become vegetarian. Her family and friends might have respected her decision or even admired her for taking a stand and adhering to her principles. But her parents complained about the fact that she wouldn't be eating the same food as them and one or two friends were upset when she would no longer join them for a burger after a night out. People may not want you to change. Beware of those who have their own interests at heart rather than yours, despite what they may say.

Our new behaviours might have all sorts of ripple effects that we hadn't anticipated. If we want to learn to **flex** for our own good we need to take account of the reactions of others so that we neither misinterpret them nor get put off.

38. Does a leopard change its spots?

flex does not erode personality; it enlarges it. Of course, some of the natural tendencies we have will remain for all sorts of reasons. They might be partially genetic, or particularly useful; they may be supported by our partner, our friends, and our family; and they may be kept in place partly by the demands of work and the context in which we live. A duchess in a stately home and a single mother working on the supermarket checkout undoubtedly inhabit completely different worlds. Each contains inbuilt habit requirements that are compatible with living successfully in those respective worlds. Individual natural tendencies and circumstances do shape each of us in the same way that the leopard's spots do. But just as a leopard does not require its *particular* pattern of spots, neither do we need to hold on to our particular habits of thinking and behaviour.

Years ago Karen sent me a passage from a letter written by Rainer Maria Rilke to a young poet who had asked him for advice. It encapsulates beautifully the notion of life having endless possibilities if we are awake to them:

> *For it is not inertia alone that is responsible for human relationships repeating themselves from case to case, indescribably monotonous and unrenewed: it is shyness before any sort of new, unforeseeable experience with which one does not think oneself able to cope. But only someone who is ready for everything, who excludes nothing, not even the most enigmatical, will live the relation to another as something alive and will himself draw exhaustively from his own existence. For if we think of this existence of the individual as a larger or smaller room, it appears evident that most people learn to know only a corner of their room, a place by the window, a strip of floor on which they walk up and down. Thus they have a certain security. And yet that dangerous insecurity is so much more human which drives the prisoners in Poe's stories to feel out the shapes of their horrible dungeons and not be strangers to the unspeakable terror of their abode. We, however, are not prisoners. No traps or snares are set about us, and there is nothing which should*

intimidate or worry us. We are set down in life as in the element to which we best correspond, and over and above this we have through thousands of years of accommodation become so like this life, that when we hold still we are, through a happy mimicry, scarcely to be distinguished from all that surrounds us. We have no reason to mistrust our world, for it is not against us. Has it terrors, they are our terrors; has it abysses, those abysses belong to us; are dangers at hand, we must try to love them.

In this passage Rilke also warns us against knowing only a corner of the room that is our existence. Imagine your life as a vast room. Why, he says, would you only want to live in one corner of it. We agree. And we urge you to explore the other 9/10ths with **flex.**

flex doesn't demand we totally change our 'personality' – just as leopards don't change their spots. The aim in **flex** is to develop and fully optimise aspects of our behavioural potential that we don't naturally use. To use more than just 1/10th of it. As Rilke says, to be 'someone who is ready for everything, who excludes nothing'. This will make us more rounded as people, more able to cope and succeed in a wider variety of circumstances, and less stressed by uncertainties we should embrace. Our natural habits make each of us rather constrained and lopsided in how we behave. They limit us to succeed only in those situations we encounter for which we happen to have the appropriate behaviours. Why would any of us choose to remain so constrained? In Rilke's terms, why would we choose to explore only a small corner of our room? What about the other 9/10ths?

Why wouldn't we Do Something Different?

flex in action – the behaviour-rater

Understanding your behaviour

The behaviour-rater

Please take your time and select any boxes that apply to you.

Firm	Unpredictable	Individually-centred	Behave as others want	Behave as you wish
Reactive	Lively	Definite	Calm/relaxed	Gentle
Plays safe	Proactive	Laid back	Open-minded	Assertive
Introverted	Systematic	Extroverted	Predictable	Conventional
Flexible	Trusting	Group-centred	Spontaneous	Risk-taker
Wary	Unconventional	Single-minded	Unassertive	Energetic/driven

Scoring your behaviour-rater

In a moment we will look at how you completed the behaviour-rater, but first notice a few things about the words in it.

None of the descriptive words or behaviours are in themselves bad or wrong or inappropriate – only a particular context might make that so.

In the table on p.60 I displayed the same words as fifteen dimensions in the sense that the descriptors might be paired at either end of a response scale. That itself often leads people to believe they are incompatible – you could not be both one and the other! But that is not so. It's quite possible – and you may well have shown this in your own responses to the behaviour-rater – to have both of the behaviours of one of the fifteen 'dimensions' in your repertoire, depending on the situations you might encounter. You can then potentially do the right thing, or the best thing, depending upon the context and your goals.

Without the entire set of behaviours this guarantee cannot be given. If you have any behaviours missing you are reducing your *chances* of being able to do the right thing by about 3 per cent for each one. If you are missing a fair number this can add up to quite a handicap. It could add up to you only using 1/10th of your potential!

And don't forget, even if you have the behaviour in your repertoire that is far from a guarantee that you will use it. Old habits die hard. Very hard. So the negatives of having a strong personality, or a narrow range of behaviours in your repertoire, are very marked indeed.

The behaviour-rater is a quick way of measuring your **flex** score. How did you do? There are two scores we can look at. The second requires a bit more work on your part.

Your behaviour range score

The first – your behaviour range score – can be simply calculated by counting up the number of boxes you ticked out of the 30 possible. Now convert that score to a percentage simply by dividing it by 30 and then multiplying the result by 100. You will get a score between 0 and 100 per cent. Most of the scores I have seen are well below 50 per cent, often in the twenties or thirties, although I have occasionally come across higher scores.

The number of descriptors you have ticked or selected gives a measure of the size and range of your 'personality' – it is an indication of what natural tendencies you see yourself as having.

Someone with a wide range of behaviours **(a high score)** is equipped with the 'Swiss Army knife' version of 'personality'. You could say they have a 'tool' for every perceivable eventuality. Ideally, a score of 100 per cent is the goal. That would indicate that a person is equipped to deal effectively with any situation and able to call upon the most appropriate behaviour. They would be able to work with and get the most from other people, see and value their strengths and adopt a variety of different perspectives.

If you have a narrow range of traits **(a low score)** this suggests you have a restricted 'toolset' for a wide range of demands and situations. That may result in your operating ineffectively, since you have fewer 'tools' at your disposal. You are trying to manage in the world using perhaps only 1/10th of your potential.

People with a low range of behaviours may find it stressful if called upon to step outside their comfort zone, generate ideas or adapt quickly to change. By increasing their behavioural flexibility and adding new behaviours to their repertoire, research shows these individuals achieve better results in their work and personal life, with less effort and less stress.

Your flex score

The second score requires you to count the number of *pairs* of behaviours you ticked.

To remind you, the pairs are:

Unassertive	Assertive
Trusting	Wary
Calm/relaxed	Energetic/driven
Reactive	Proactive
Definite	Flexible
Risk-taker	Plays safe
Behave as others want	Behave as you wish
Spontaneous	Systematic
Single-minded	Open-minded
Introverted	Extroverted
Conventional	Unconventional
Individually-centred	Group-centred
Firm	Gentle
Lively	Laid back
Predictable	Unpredictable

Only count a pair if you ticked *both* of them. There are 15 pairs, so take your score and divide it by 15 and multiply the result by 100. This will give you another number between 0 and 100 per cent. On this score it is not uncommon to get zero, and most people score about 15 per cent – i.e. two to three pairs ticked out of fifteen.

Most people score much less than 50 per cent, even though 100 per cent is achievable on both the behaviour range score and the flex score.

Interpreting your behaviour-rater score

I can hear complaints from some of you. Some of you will be feeling a little cheated. Don't forget that feeling because I will be coming back to it. Some of you will be saying that you did not realise you could tick the opposites! Others may be saying you have more behaviours in your repertoire than you ticked but they are not representative of how you *normally* behave (or something like that).

Perhaps some of you behave differently at home, or with your partner, than you do at work or with your boss and you have not represented these nuances in your answers. Yes, that is likely. But your scores do represent something about you and you need to reflect upon that feeling of being cheated because that might be a barrier to change.

I have often found the most inflexible successful people are the ones who most strongly 'defend' themselves when they score less than they expect. I have FIT profiled many CEOs and senior managers, Premier League football managers, top financiers and the like. These are successful people. And successful people like to believe they are successful because the way they behave is the best way to win. But there are many routes to success for talented people. And it is likely that other routes would make them even more successful, or successful with less sweat, or less collateral damage to themselves (less stress, perhaps?) and those around them (less unhappy families, perhaps?). We are all, after all, habitual about how we behave and will defend ourselves.

Our academic research shows that individuals who develop a wide range of attributes find it easier to make decisions, handle different situations better, cope well with change and generally get more from life.

The behaviour-rater is, of course, just a simple and quick test to get you to think about your behaviours.

flex yourself – Do Something Different

Look at your behaviour-rater. Which behaviours didn't you tick? If you tend to behave more one way than the other you may have an asymmetric personality.

Yes, you could be psychologically lopsided. Most of us are.

Since we only use part of our personality, that part becomes strong and muscular and the other 90 per cent, if you're not careful, can wither away and die from lack of use! **flex** is a way of changing that and of putting that other 90 per cent to work for you.

The way to **flex** yourself is to start trying out some behaviours associated with the opposite of your often-used trait; literally experiment with another way of being. Just once or twice, or for one day, perhaps. Remember, there are no rights or wrongs, no good or bad here. All ways of behaving can be equally acceptable depending on the circumstances. The key is being able to act in the most appropriate way given the demands of the situation, not habitually reacting without thinking in the same old way. A good way to start is to experiment with some of the behaviours you don't usually use. To start **flex**ing yourself in small ways. You will find some **flex**ing ideas below. No one's saying you've got to undergo a radical personality change; you've just got to try *not* being yourself now and again. See how it feels. Notice the response you get from others. Remember the law of unintended consequences – good things that you didn't expect may come back to you.

Look at the behaviours on the next few pages. Select the ones you *didn't* tick on your behaviour-rater and try out some of the suggestions associated with that trait. It's doing something different again, but this time with your personality.

The unassertive–assertive dimension

Unassertive? Try being more assertive.

- Speak up when you would normally hold back.
- Be direct in asking for what you want.
- Express an opinion.
- Be more forceful in putting something across you believe in.
- Say no (when it's OK to).
- Refuse a request without giving a reason or excuses.
- Suggest a trip out to the person closest to you.
- Write a short letter to the local newspaper about something that's important to you.
- Practise saying, 'I don't agree with that.'
- When questioned today, be decisive in your answer even if you feel unsure.
- Next time you disagree with something you see on the Internet, voice your opinion in the feedback.
- If you don't like a haircut/meal/purchase then send it back, complain or return it.
- Don't take no for an answer today.

Assertive? Try being more unassertive.

- Stay in the background more.
- Ignore criticism; don't react.
- Behave as if another person knows better than you.
- Let somebody else decide or choose something for you.
- Practise saying, 'I'll go with the flow.'
- Say a lot less than you would normally do.
- Try saying, 'I don't mind, you choose.'
- Ask someone, 'Is there anything I can do to help?'
- Ask someone to suggest a trip somewhere.

- Even when you think you know the answer, ask someone else's opinion and see how it contrasts with your own.
- Let your partner/friend choose what to do on your next night out.
- When eating out ask someone for a recommendation and try it.

The trusting–wary dimension

Trusting? Try being more wary.

- Ask for a reason why.
- Check the facts carefully.
- Find out about someone else from others.
- Check out if people are who they say they are.
- Be more mysterious.
- Update or change your privacy settings and passwords.
- Google people you know and find out more about them.
- Keep a secret diary.
- Cover your tracks.
- Find a secret hideaway place for your special things.
- Go on holiday but don't tell too many people where.
- Find an opportunity to say, 'I'll think about it' instead of, 'Yes, OK.'
- Check the other options before agreeing to something.
- Do some background research before diving into something new.

Wary? Try being more trusting.

- Don't ask for reasons why.
- Allow someone to do things their own way.
- Let another person make a decision for you.
- Tell someone a secret.
- Disclose something personal about yourself in public.
- Make friends with someone online.

- Start a public blog relating all you do.
- Practise saying, 'Go ahead, I trust you.'
- Put all your treasures on display to the world.
- Invite anyone who wants to join you on holiday.
- The next time someone suggests something fun (and safe!), give it a go.
- Try delegating a job to a colleague/friend/family member.
- Play the game where you fall backwards into someone's arms, then return the favour.
- Have a shower with your eyes closed.
- Let someone do something that you think you can do better.

The calm/relaxed–energetic/driven dimension

Calm and relaxed? Try being more energetic and driven.

- Take on a new role or activity.
- Take 20 per cent less time over everything you do.
- Do something you've been putting off for a long while.
- Take some initiative when you'd normally leave it to somebody else.
- Exercise first thing in the morning to raise your energy levels.
- Set yourself deadlines for everything you do.
- Walk somewhere you'd normally take the car/bus/taxi.
- Walk up and down the stairs just for the sake of it.
- Fix something that needs fixing.
- Cook something new when you would normally order in.
- Practise saying, 'I'll do it straight away' (and mean it).
- Take up a hobby that's fast-paced.
- List five things that need doing – then do them today.

Energetic and driven? Try being more calm and relaxed.

- Take five minutes' time out just to think, once an hour, every hour.
- Do something really slowly instead of rushing through it.
- Put something off until later.
- Let go, of others and the outside world, and focus only on things you *can* control.
- Let yourself be bored – don't fight it.
- Imagine you have staff who will take care of everything for you.
- Go for a walk somewhere nice and think about the word 'relax'.
- Imagine a summer's day and that you're a bird flying from one place to another.
- Hide from someone until they notice you're not there.
- Write down three things that make you feel relaxed and positive.
- Practise meditation/breathing slowly.
- Put a picture or phrase that relaxes you in a place where you'll see it.
- Close your eyes at least once today and visualise a favourite place.
- Go out for a fifteen-minute aimless stroll today.

The reactive–proactive dimension

Reactive? Try being more proactive.

- Take the initiative.
- Carry out some research to support a future decision.
- Learn a skill you might need in the future.
- Express a feeling that will start or alter a relationship.
- Put a strategy in place.
- Prepare a prenuptial agreement.
- Do something that will repay you in five, ten or twenty years' time.
- Investigate a prepaid funeral plan.
- Ask yourself, 'How can I be better prepared for what's to come?'

- Write a letter to yourself in the future.

- Get Christmas organised before the end of August.

- Find out about/take up a new form of exercise.

- Plan the meals you will eat for the next week.

- Run a personal health check on yourself. Do something that will improve your long-term health.

- Ring a person you have not spoken to for a while; surprise them.

- Buy cards/presents for the next three events (e.g. birthdays, anniversaries) coming up.

- Stock up a first-aid kit and learn a first-aid technique.

- Do a safety/security check on your home (fire extinguishers, smoke alarms, window locks, carbon monoxide detectors).

Proactive? Try being more reactive.

- Let another person take the initiative.

- Express how you feel in the moment.

- Go with the flow on something.

- Commit to someone on the spur of the moment.

- Express your first reactions to someone.

- Indulge in some instant gratification.

- Dance or sing along when you hear a song you like, wherever you are.

- Respond to the weather, however it makes you feel.

- Wait for the other person to call instead of always taking the lead.

- If you are unsure about something, don't act; wait and see how you really feel.

- Reply to a letter or request without delaying.

- Practise saying, 'This is how I feel about that right now.'

The definite–flexible dimension

Definite? Try being more flexible.

- Let someone sell you something small you'd already decided against.
- Ask yourself how it seems from the other person's point of view, e.g. how you interact at the supermarket checkout, or how you reply to an issue your partner raises.
- On the hour each hour, stop before you do what you are naturally going to do next. Could you try something different that might be more beneficial?
- Try someone else's suggestion instead of your own.
- Let others be 'right' today.
- Ask for advice from someone around you whom you can't remember asking advice from before.
- Practise saying, 'It's up to you.'
- Ask for advice from someone in a shop.
- Listen to a radio station you know you don't like.
- Change your routine; do three things today that you wouldn't normally do.
- Act according to an alternative view to one you have held for a long time.
- Let others be themselves; don't question or criticise them.
- Turn a blind eye to some usual household chores today.

Flexible? Try being more definite.

- Take a stance and see the benefits of a firm line.
- Be less accommodating (when you think it is appropriate).
- Make a strategic decision and act on it.
- Pay more attention to the big issues; don't be distracted by the smaller details.
- Stick to a choice and don't change your mind.

- Imagine you are a brand and invent a personal slogan.
- Answer the question, 'Where is all this activity taking me?'
- Imagine what it's like to be right most of the time.
- Be tougher with someone than you normally are.
- Make a decision that you've been putting off for a long while.
- Ask yourself, 'What would I do if I was in charge?'
- Set a new house rule and stick to it.

The risk-taker–plays safe dimension

Risk-taker? Try playing safe more.

- Check all the facts before doing something.
- Have a back-up plan in case things go wrong.
- Work out fully what could go wrong, and what to do about it.
- Add up all the costs of doing the things you do.
- Ask yourself, 'What would my parents want me to do?'
- Check out the fine print in all your insurance policies.
- Get things in writing.
- Reserve judgement before offering an opinion.
- Wait until you know someone before committing to anything.
- Practise saying, 'What are the guarantees?'
- Plan your days according to the long-range weather forecast.
- Before deciding to try something new, get the opinion of three friends.
- Seek out someone who has expertise in the area before trying something new.
- Fill up your car before it gets anywhere near empty.
- Have your boiler or car serviced.

- Put some money away for a rainy day.

Play safe? Try taking more risk.

- Have a flutter – place an affordable bet.
- Tell someone what you think of them.
- Challenge a fear or phobia.
- Do something where there are no guarantees.
- Take up an extreme sport.
- Wear a T-shirt with a provocative slogan.
- Ask people what they honestly think of you.
- Plan a barbecue on a day when rain is forecast.
- Leave your underwear off and cross a busy street.
- Face a fear today, no matter how small.
- Single? Invite someone who appeals to you out on a date.
- Practise saying, 'What's the worst that could happen?'
- Go to a restaurant and order something you have never heard of.
- If you're single, ask a friend you trust to set you up on a blind date.
- Go to a club/event/film on your own.
- Introduce yourself to a neighbour you haven't met.

The behave as others want–behave as you wish dimension

Behave as others want? Try behaving as you wish.

- Don't go along with someone else's suggestion.
- Plan an evening around what you enjoy doing.
- Choose a different option to the rest of the group.
- Put a long-lived secret dream into action.
- Be the one who stands out and speaks up.
- Keep a journal of your wishes – and your goals.
- Email your Amazon wish list to all your friends.

- If you have children tell them not to bother you all weekend.
- Dress differently to how you normally do.
- Arrange to go to that pop concert you always wanted to go to.
- Suggest a night out for family or friends and get everyone on board.
- Don't let others' reactions affect you taking a decision, if it's right.
- Spot your people-pleasing habit today and ask yourself, 'Who am I doing this for?'

Behave as you wish? Try behaving as others want.

- Do something you know your parents would approve of.
- Ask another what you should do.
- Let someone else make plans for you.
- Be the last to take a seat or join a queue.
- Join that Facebook group.
- Play a game with your children (or grandchildren) if you have them.
- Say yes to the next thing someone asks you to do.
- Ask yourself, 'What would my friends want me to do?'
- If you have children, let them plan the whole weekend.
- Let a friend decide your next night out.
- Ask your boss for three ways you can improve your work; try them.
- Try dressing like other people at work; how does it feel?
- Next time someone says something you disagree with, agree anyway.
- Behave at least once today in a way you know others would approve of.

The spontaneous–systematic dimension

Spontaneous? Try being more systematic.

- Make a plan of action for the next two days.
- Organise an area of your life that's too haphazard, e.g. sort out your CDs or photos, put your finances in order, etc.

- List the things you want to achieve in the next week, next year and in your life. Plan how you will reach these goals and the steps you will take.

- Timetable your whole day in half-hour slots.

- Imagine your strictest school teacher is running your life.

- Tidy up something that needs tidying up.

- Arrange to meet up with a friend you haven't seen for a while.

- Stop and ask yourself, 'how can I do this systematically?'

- Decide on three things you're going to do tomorrow and then do them.

- Plan a holiday for next year; make all the arrangements you can.

- Sort out that pile of paperwork you've been ignoring.

- Pick a room in your house that needs attention and draw up an action plan.

- Compare your bank balance now with a year ago. Work out what changes to make.

Systematic? Try being more spontaneous.

- Do something on the spur of the moment.

- Ignore your plans and just do what feels right.

- Try something silly or frivolous – just for fun.

- Phone an old friend out of the blue.

- Let the day unfold without organising it; just see what happens.

- Turn up at your local cinema and watch the next film that's starting.

- Surf the net and express your views somewhere.

- Invite someone to dance, wherever you are.

- Practise saying, 'Let's do it!'

- Ask yourself what tomorrow would be like if there was no plan.

- Go to bed an hour later or earlier than normal, whichever is more unusual.

- On a walk toss a coin each time you can choose which way to go: heads go left, tails go right.

- List six options for a night out; roll a dice to decide.
- Stick a pin in a map – make the destination your next road trip.
- Drop everything and invite a friend or colleague to go for a coffee.
- Replace one of today's tasks with something more fun.

The single-minded–open-minded dimension

Single-minded? Try being more open-minded.

- Seek the advice of a person much younger than you.
- Instead of rejecting an idea, ask 'Why?' or 'Why not?'
- Mix with people who don't share your views or background.
- Look for areas of agreement during conversation.
- Try a new sexual position/practice.
- Expose yourself to music/food/customs of another culture.
- Plan a trip somewhere unusual and different.
- Read a blog on a topic that challenges your views. Look for points of agreement and leave a comment.
- Ask yourself, 'Am I jumping to conclusions here?'
- Get as many opinions as you can before making an important decision.
- Stop and chat to the next charity worker that stops you in the street.
- Practise saying, 'That's different to how I see it. Tell me more.'
- Find out about the views of a political party you disagree with.

Open-minded? Try being more single-minded.

- Don't consult others when you know what needs to be done.
- Speak up for the underdog or refuse to listen to gossip.
- Campaign for something you feel strongly about.
- Stop being your parents' 'child'.

- Scrutinise your views – are they your own?

- Ask yourself, 'What do I really believe in?'

- Drop a custom that's been handed down from the past.

- Do not be swayed by the popular view.

- If you know how you feel, do not listen to the opinion of others.

- Practise saying, 'I don't mind if others don't agree with me.'

The introverted–extroverted dimension

Introverted? Try being more extroverted.

- Contribute to a discussion when you wouldn't normally express your opinion. Speak up and make yourself heard.

- Make the first move in a friendship situation, e.g. plan a party or organise a get-together with friends.

- Get out of your shell, e.g. talk to somebody new or somebody you meet at an event.

- Draw a little more attention to yourself; introduce yourself/tell a joke.

- Create an online identity and ask people to become fans.

- Have an 'open house' for all your neighbours at home.

- Find somewhere where you can shout and then shout the first word that comes into your head as loud as you can.

- Say hello to someone you've never said hello to before.

- Practise telling a funny story; embellish it for effect.

- Go commando (i.e. don't wear any pants) or wear crazy socks or a hat.

- Start a conversation with three strangers today.

- Practise saying, 'Are we having fun?' (but don't be too annoying!)

- Find out the names of people you see regularly but never really speak to (shopkeepers, till workers, people at the train station).

- Organise a night out at a karaoke bar; put your name down first to sing.

- Ask yourself, 'What would my most outgoing friend do?'

Extroverted? Experiment with being more introverted.

- Listen more and speak less.
- Spend some time alone; enjoy your own company.
- Say no to a social invitation.
- Let yourself fade into the background a bit more.
- Don't interrupt other people or finish their sentences.
- Keep your opinions to yourself.
- Get together with a small group of special friends.
- Stop yourself from talking on three occasions during the day.
- Describe your innermost feelings in a poem but don't share it.
- Listen to a conversation you're not involved in and repeat one sentence to yourself three times.
- Imagine how you'd feel if you were shipwrecked alone on an island.
- Practise saying, 'I would like to be alone for a while.'
- Spend time alone at home without the TV or radio on.
- Stay off Facebook; resist the temptation to scrutinise other people's lives for a while.

The conventional–unconventional dimension

Conventional? Try being more unconventional.

- Look at situations from a completely different angle, e.g. as a teenager, a foreigner or an alien might.
- Wear something different and daring.
- Take something in your life that's very ordinary and change it, e.g. your voicemail message, choice of food or décor.
- Look at what others are doing and be different.
- Buy yourself a treat – from a toy shop.
- Voice a radical opinion.
- Create an online identity for your pet and voice its opinions.

- Add a few rogue ingredients to a standard recipe.
- Take a photo of yourself looking as unconventional as you can manage.
- Say what your name is, how old you are and where you live in a foreign accent. Record it and play it back, if you can. Do it again in a different accent.
- Swear out loud.
- Take an alternative route to work or if possible work different hours for a week.
- Wave at a stranger on a passing bus.
- Stand in front of the mirror and spend two minutes talking gibberish.
- Pull a funny face whenever you pass a mirror or window.

Unconventional? Try being more conventional.

- Make the more conventional choice rather than having to be different.
- Consider the more traditional alternative.
- Conform and take the most common option.
- Agree with someone even if you don't share their view.
- Do something that's really traditional.
- Observe an old local custom and share with your neighbours.
- Cook a very old recipe.
- Hold doors open for people.
- Sing the national anthem.
- Call someone 'sir' or 'madam' (as appropriate).
- Give up your seat on public transport.
- Take a photo of yourself looking as conventional as you can manage.
- Talk about the weather a lot.
- Dress more conservatively.
- Spend a day trying to be un-cool.

- Have a conversation with your parent(s) and agree with everything they say.
- Do not swear all day.
- Be extremely polite with everyone you meet.

The individually-centred–group-centred dimension

Individually-centred? Try being more group-centred.

- Ask other group members what you can do for the group.
- Offer support or help to another group member.
- Initiate a chat with one or more of your group about the needs of the group.
- Organise something that all of the group can take part in.
- Be willing to learn from family and friends; remain open to the suggestions of others.
- Help a stranger.
- Practise saying, 'Is everybody here happy?'
- Donate some money to charity (any amount is OK).
- Organise a board game with at least three other people.
- Volunteer some of your time to a worthy cause.
- Plan a surprise for a friend's birthday that is approaching.
- Before making a decision today – find out what others want.
- Take a family vote on decisions, e.g. holiday, film-watching, decorating.
- Find out if others think you are doing your fair share around the house.

Group-centred? Try being more individually-centred.

- Take an individual stance (when it's appropriate to do so).
- Share your individual needs with one or more members of the group.
- Do the right thing without asking others.

- Do something purely for yourself.

- Buy yourself a treat or send yourself flowers.

- Tell the rest of the group what isn't working for you.

- Find a quiet spot where you won't be disturbed and read twenty-five pages of a book.

- Practise saying, 'My needs are just as important as other people's.'

- Make or buy yourself your favourite meal.

- Set aside thirty minutes for 'me time'. Listen to music, read a book, do what you like.

- When you do something well, congratulate yourself.

- Decide on tonight's meal without asking others what they want.

The firm–gentle dimension

Firm? Try being gentler.

- Sympathise without trying to solve the problem.

- Show your vulnerable side.

- Don't push; wait and see what happens.

- Write a letter of sympathy or apology.

- Learn the words of a poem by heart.

- Be the first to say sorry.

- Give more hugs.

- Ask yourself, 'What would Mother Theresa have done?'

- Put yourself in someone else's shoes before judging them.

- Make a CD of love songs.

- Listen to someone without interrupting or offering an opinion.

- Offer to help someone in need.

- Practise saying, 'Let's take this slowly.'

- Whisper at your children today (instead of raising your voice).

- Smile broadly instead of speaking out.

Gentle? Try being firmer.

- Take a stance on something you won't put up with.
- Try raising your voice a little.
- Practise using phrases that are more definite.
- Repeat your wishes if you are not being heard.
- Write a letter of complaint or rant publicly.
- Ask yourself, 'What would Alan Sugar do?'
- Do not apologise for being yourself.
- Send back a meal, or goods, that you aren't happy with.
- Offer your opinion in a situation you normally wouldn't.
- Practise saying, 'This is something I feel very strongly about.'
- Cut ties with anyone who makes you feel bad/uses you.
- Report bad service you have received.

The lively–laid back dimension

Lively? Try being more laid back.

- Stay a little longer.
- Stop and examine the detail.
- Take up a relaxing hobby.
- Make vague plans; turn up when you feel like it.
- Close your eyes and think something through in detail.
- Don't rush; take the scenic route.
- Let the day unfold without organising it.
- Ask yourself, 'What would the Dalai Lama do?'
- Leave your watch or mobile phone at home for a day.
- Listen to a relaxation CD.
- Do not set your alarm at the weekend; lie in.
- Stay at home and read a book instead of going out.
- Practise saying, 'Let's just chill.'

Laid back? Try being livelier.

- Get some of tomorrow's activities done today.
- Turn off the television.
- Find a shortcut.
- Stop labouring over something and finish quickly.
- Draw up a really ambitious to-do list – and do it!
- Ask yourself, 'What would Jamie Oliver do?'
- Stand up and walk about instead of sitting.
- Join a gym or sign up for a weekly class.
- Go running.
- Get up earlier and get a chore done before work.
- Volunteer your time.
- Practise saying, 'Let's do it!'
- Time yourself doing a regular daily chore. Try to improve on your time.

The predictable–unpredictable dimension

Predictable? Try being more unpredictable.

- Make changes to your morning routine.
- Suggest something that wouldn't be expected from you.
- Do something that's not age-appropriate.
- Just say, 'F*ck it!' and do it.
- Just turn up at a party or an event.
- Ask everyone to call you by a different name for a day.
- Say something that people wouldn't expect of you.
- Don't turn up when expected to/drift in later or earlier than expected.
- Wear something that is not your normal style.
- Hang out with people much older or younger than you.
- Go to bed earlier/later than you would normally.

- Practise saying, 'You'll have to wait and see!'
- Surprise a loved one with a special treat.

Unpredictable? Try being more predictable.

- Set a regular time for calling a friend or relative.
- Automatise a healthy habit (e.g. savings, check-ups).
- Keep a promise.
- Stick to a deadline.
- Don't give the response that everyone expects of you.
- Imagine your life as if it was stage-managed.
- Use the alarm on your phone for everything you plan to do today.
- Turn up exactly on time.
- Make a weekly plan; organise your life.
- Try to go to bed at the same time every day for a week.
- Get your paperwork in order and set a day each month to keep it organised.
- Send friends a goodnight text at the same time every night.
- Decide how you will react to certain issues/people and stick to it.

3

Section 3:
Doing something different,
personal coherence and
decision-making

39. Do Something Different

By now I hope the notion that we are habit machines and need to behave more flexibly makes intuitive sense to you. FIT identifies the traits and behavioural dimensions that make life less stressful and help us to get what we want. But how do we actually go about making the changes? How do we put FIT into practice? The fact that people are generally habit-bound, resistant to new experiences and have narrow behavioural repertoires might lead you to think that change is virtually impossible. It needn't be!

That is why we have distilled a complex problem down to one simple solution. Do Something Different works because it involves doing things every day that take us just outside the usual comfort zone. And trying small tasks that are fun but that go against the grain of our normal habits. It also helps create new behaviours that expand our usual repertoire. We think it is groundbreaking and those who've tried it agree with us.

Behaviour change is a huge topic these days. In 2010 BJ Fogg of Stanford University's *Persuasive Technology Lab* released a list of the top ten mistakes in behaviour change. His list is reproduced in the table below and explains why most self-help books miss the point. We think that Do Something Different avoids each of these mistakes as follows:

	Stanford University's Top 10 Mistakes in Behaviour Change	How Do Something Different (DSD) Avoids Each Mistake
1	Relying on willpower for long-term change	*DSD adds things to life and isn't depriving; hence it is fun and there is no need for willpower.*
2	Attempting big leaps instead of baby steps	*DSD is based on small, manageable micro-steps.*
3	Ignoring how environment shapes behaviours	*DSD subtly changes the person's environment and gives them control over it.*
4	Trying to stop old behaviours instead of creating new ones	*DSD wholly aims to create new behaviours.*
5	Blaming failures on lack of motivation	*DSD operates on the principle that failures come from the pull of old habits and have little to do with motivation.*
6	Underestimating the power of triggers	*DSD tackles all the small daily habits that trigger unwanted behaviour.*

(Continued over page)

	Stanford University's Top 10 Mistakes in Behaviour Change	How Do Something Different (DSD) Avoids Each Mistake
7	Believing that information leads to action	DSD does not rely on informing, educating or incentivising.
8	Focusing on abstract goals more than concrete behaviours	Concrete behaviours are the stock-in-trade of DSD.
9	Seeking at the outset to change the behaviour forever	DSD starts by encouraging small changes in the person. These small steps reward the person so they want to take bigger ones.
10	Believing that behaviour change is always difficult	Behaviour change can be easy with DSD.

40. What does a Do Something Different intervention look like?

We know that when people keep doing the same things it can make life at best boring and at worst troublesome. But habits also narrow our view. They blind us to the many other options that are available to us. Therefore a Do Something Different programme simply suggests different things to do each day. These switch off the person's autopilot and put them back in the driving seat of life. By making small daily disruptions to their everyday life they start to steer it down a different track. There's no struggle, no gritted teeth to maintain willpower – just a gradual loosening of the habit-web that had a stranglehold on the person.

In this way Do Something Different circumvents people's natural resistance to change. It chips away at their inertia. It can be integrated into their daily routine and most importantly it doesn't require willpower because the changes are small.

When a person starts to Do Something Different they:

- expand their world
- break free of the comfort zone
- shake off the habits that held them back
- look at things differently
- open up to new possibilities
- see themselves in a new light
- allow new opportunities into their life and
- have different reflections about themselves.

Our programmes contain a number of specially selected DSDs. Often they are designed with a special life-goal or transformation in mind. But they all tend to fall into the following categories:

Disruptors
These break habit chains. They disrupt automatic unthinking patterns of behaviour that cause people to do things without thinking or intending to.

Expanders

These enlarge people's behavioural repertoire, expand existing thinking and behavioural patterns, and bring about new reflections.

View-changers

These shift the way people view themselves and their lives, giving a different perspective and helping them see things in a non-habitual way.

You may have already tried some of the DSDs in this book. Have a look below at some of the daily DSDs from *Do Something Different: The Journal*. A lot of people use them as reminders of how life can be shaken up and stirred for the better!

Remember that these are not big, demanding life-changes – they only have to be tried for *one single day*. But each one can lead to long-term changes, as small disruptions can cause big differences. And the cumulative effect of doing them all over time can lead to huge personal change and transformation. Here are a few examples, and a brief explanation of why they work:

- SHIFT YOUR BUTT DAY: Today, don't sit anywhere that you would normally sit. That's at the dining table, at work, watching TV or in a meeting.

  Triggers for unwanted behaviour often exist in our daily routines and the environment around us. Literally changing where we sit can mean we are not triggered to do what we would normally do in that place.

- LET GO OF TIME DAY: Don't use a watch or a clock today. See how good you are at time-keeping or just relax and try not letting time run your life.

  Letting go of external props that 'run' our life can give us a different perspective on it and put us back in control.

- BREAK RANKS DAY: Swap a job/chore with your partner or friend today. Get some insight into their life by doing something they do.

  Relationship habits get entrenched and cause problems when people cannot take the other's perspective.

- LONG TIME NO SEE DAY: Rekindle an old friendship today. Make sure it's a quality one that you miss; you may have let it slip away but today take steps to renew it.

  Many people let things like good friendships drift away. This DSD pushes them to get back in control.

- SPRUCE UP DAY: Experiment with your image today. Wear something you wouldn't normally wear and break free from your wardrobe rut. If you're a jeans/trouser wearer, wear a skirt. Men who are always formal – go on, undo that top button!

  People's sartorial habits imprison them and put them in a box. How we present ourselves to the world can affect how we behave and how we are perceived. This DSD can be the catalyst for changing that.

- FEEL THE PINCH DAY: Go out without any money today. Of course, make sure the car has petrol and take some food, but then see what you can get for nothing. Free entry to museums, music downloads, discarded newspapers, tasting samples…

  Forcing ourselves into the discomfort zone – in this case a day without money – can trigger all kinds of new feelings and experiences. Not depending on money on this particular day makes us look around for alternatives and raises awareness.

- GIVE AWAY DAY: Give somebody a small present today. If you haven't any money then give a cuddle, a compliment or just cheer up someone who's going through a rough time.

  When friendships or relationships become habitual we stop putting in the effort. Or get into the habit of waiting for another to take the initiative. This DSD forces a small interpersonal shift in the right direction. Who knows where it might lead?

- NEW NEWS DAY: Change your newspaper today – buy one you would never normally consider buying. If you don't usually take one, then do so today. Notice how the media portrays the news, and shapes your views.

A really simple DSD but a powerful view-changer too. We also encourage people to read their usual newspaper in a different order (back to front?) or focus on sections they usually skip. Or to buy a hobby magazine about something in which they think they have no interest whatsoever!

- THAT'LL DO DAY: Be less of a perfectionist today. Try saying 'That'll do' when you've finished a job and stop gilding the lily. If perfectionism is preventing you from starting something, tell yourself, 'I don't have to get it right, I just have to get it going.'

  *Behavioural habits and traits like perfectionism render us inflexible. They trap us into filling our life with the wrong things and the wrong worries. This DSD gives the perfectionist permission to **flex** a little. A good stress-buster.*

- STRETCH YOUR HORIZONS DAY: Investigate a different type of holiday – search for ethical/adventurous or hobby holidays and expand your vacation view! Why not go somewhere different – with someone different?

  Habits are not just daily; they can happen once a year as with holidays. A new environment can be the catalyst for a whole range of new experiences.

- STOP COMPLAINING DAY: Have a no-moan day today. Whenever you find yourself about to whinge or criticise, say something positive – or just smile instead!

  A DSD to interrupt a habit that many slip into – complaining. It's easy to do but it's also infectious and corrosive. It's one that if not broken will affect how the person perceives and shapes their world.

41. How does Do Something Different work?

Experiencing and reflecting selves

Why does doing something different work? Remember we are all much more than our conscious thoughts and the utterances we make, whether these be right or wrong. Our habits are examples of the unconscious forces that drive our behaviour. Where the autopilot is taking us may not be what we would choose for ourselves. It just … well, happened.

Sigmund Freud made a career from this fact. He was among the first to notice the disconnection between what we think and what we do. In this sense, we are at least two selves in one body. Freud thought we were three, and labelled these the id, the ego and the superego. Of course, many of his ideas have been debunked and superseded by modern knowledge of how the brain functions. But a model we find useful is to see people in terms of their *experiencing self* and their *reflecting self*, shown in Figure 4. When we are coherent these two selves are not in conflict with each other. Do Something Different brings about this coherence.

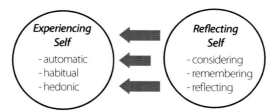

The *experiencing self* is our online experience as it happens. It includes how we automatically feel and think at the time we are doing something. It's where our habits reside.

The *reflecting self* is our concept of ourselves, our memories and the way we see, and want to see, ourselves in the past and future.

An incoherent individual's experiences (what they do) are at odds with their reflections (what they say or what they really want). In stressed or inflexible people the two can be poles apart.

42. Interactions between the two selves

There can be various interactions between the experiencing self and the reflecting self:

The *experiencing self* functions most of the time without effort. As the source of our habitual behaviours it is influenced heavily by automatic triggers and the demands of gratification. These habitual automatic processes drive our thoughts and behaviours and these forces often have the upper hand in determining what we think and do at any point in time. This self uses fewer of the brain's resources.

The *reflecting self* remembers what we have done before and what our intentions are. It can influence what we do by exerting effort and conscious control. It may contribute to our feelings at the time by automatic reactions (of guilt, for example, if we are experiencing something our reflecting self knows is bad for us).

Effort is needed to allow our reflecting self to take charge of what we do in the moment. At times of incoherence – when the natural needs of the experiencing self are at odds with the reflecting self – this is especially important. These are times when the person can lapse back into habit and hedonism. However, they are also the times when developmental and **flex** growth potential is greatest. Also, people often try to justify the actions of the experiencing self and in so doing may reveal their incoherence. But if there is coherence between the experiencing and reflecting self, the person will usually seem to be unstressed, comfortable and sorted.

43. Experiencing and reflecting on our own development

This distinction between our experiencing and reflecting selves is fundamental to understanding how we can achieve personal coherence. It is also key to knowing how we can succeed in making desired changes. Beneficial change cannot happen without changes to both the experiencing and the reflecting self.

Most personal development programmes and behaviour change interventions fail to do this. This is shown in Figure 5 below.

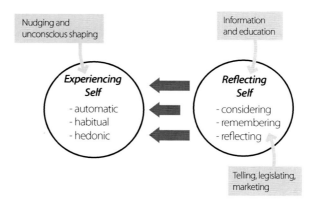

Most programmes aim at either the experiencing self or at the reflecting self but don't affect both. For example, information and education target the reflecting self. They try to change people's thoughts and intentions, but that often doesn't affect experience. People know what they should do but don't do it. Another technique, nudging, has caught people's attention lately. This involves changing the way choices are presented to make the best one easier to choose. For example, many people fail to register as organ donors even though they would be willing to give their organs after death. A 'nudge' technique might involve making it easy for you to tick a box to register, for example, when applying for a new driving licence or passport. People might also be 'nudged' to eat more healthily if fruit and vegetables are the first choices displayed when queueing for food in a canteen. So nudging involves unconsciously manipulating environmental triggers to make certain behaviours more likely. It targets the experiencing self and tries to influence people's immediate experience. However, the reflecting self largely remains unaffected.

We have found that people cannot change for the good without tackling both the experiencing and the reflecting self. Personal development has to alter the way we experience ourselves and our world. It also has to alter our repertoire of behaviours and the way we react to things. Without both these elements changes will be neither permanent nor helpful.

44. The 'golden rules' for behaviour change

We propose that for personal change to be effective and sustainable, change has to occur in both the experiencing and the reflecting self. Targeting only one might make a short-term difference but will be ineffective in the long term. The following conditions for change interventions are necessary because they affect both selves. They need to:

- be pleasurable and relatively pain-free for the person
- bring short-term effects or rewards
- provide novel experiences that expand the person
- reshape future attitudes, memories and beliefs
- reduce the power of previous habits and
- develop a new, broader set of behaviours/cognitions for the person.

Do Something Different satisfies all these conditions and this is illustrated in Figure 6.

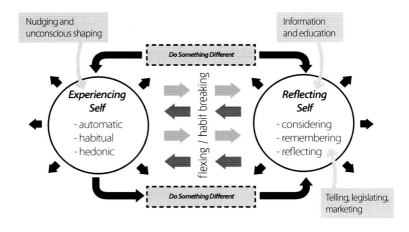

The Do Something Different tasks in our programmes are designed to:

- be fun and pleasurable, aiming to minimise the pain of change – by breaking change down into small daily things to do, the rewards and feedback should also be immediate

- challenge the person to try something new and unfamiliar, and thereby expand them so they use more of their personality

- reshape their future thoughts by gradually changing the core of the person

- weaken the pull of old habits

- incrementally add new behaviours and cognitions to the person's repertoire and

- enable the person to **flex** and get more from life.

45. Bringing about long-term behaviour change

If you are somebody who wants to change, or just improve, your life you may be confronted or even confused by the plethora of self-help and personal development programmes around. But when making a choice these are some of the key points to bear in mind:

- **Does the change process rely on willpower?**

  If so there is a high likelihood that most people will fail most of the time. The most successful personal change frameworks only work when they reduce the demand for willpower.

  Do Something Different does not require willpower; the emphasis is not on depriving yourself but on adding something to your life.

- **Can the changes be easily integrated into everyday living?**

  If not, there's not likely to be much change. That's because constant effort will be needed to keep up the new behaviours and this will wane over time (and at the end of each day!).

  Do Something Different works on the basis of daily behaviour changes – small, achievable and fun things that can be done in the course of daily life.

- **Is just one behaviour being targeted for change?**

  Most people try to just change one thing. For example, if a person wants to lose weight, they may embark on a diet but won't also tackle habits in their relationships, their stress levels, and in their engagement with life generally. For that very reason, failure is likely. Without broader changes the target behaviour will continue to be supported by existing habits.

  Do Something Different programmes address all the habits in a person's life, since even apparently unrelated habits can maintain unwanted behaviour.

- **Does the change framework require the person to keep the specific target goal in mind?**

  If so, this will work against success for two reasons:

  1. Having to constantly keep the goal in the conscious mind demands constant cognitive effort that will prove too demanding in the long term.

  2. Having a constant focus on the target can lead to 'behavioural rebound'. Thinking constantly about not doing something (e.g. smoking, eating unhealthily) makes the doing of it more likely, not less. The brain is conditioned to seek out that which it is deprived of (so the dieter is more sensitive to food cues than the non-dieter).

  Do Something Different engages the person in new enjoyable behaviours, distracting them from those things they should not be doing. It is the tool with which we increase flexibility and bring about coherence in the person.

46. Coherence comes from doing the right thing

Doing the right thing is more than making a decision or deploying a behaviour that works in a given situation. To do the right thing means doing the thing that is right *for you*. In the book so far we have described the personal ingredients that make it possible for a person to be successful (the dimensions and constancies in FIT Science and the need to **flex** and DSD).

But just doing lots of different things is not in itself enough.

Being excessively flexible and elastic may take you away from what you want, not closer to it, because you are veering around all over the place! Behaviour has to be shaped and directed towards the right thing. But how do you know what the right thing is for you?

First, there is no universal 'right thing'. And doing what is right for you may be different from doing what is right for me. That stems from our very individuality. And it goes to the core of who we are.

Consider the intriguing question of why so many people seem to do the wrong thing so predictably and so often. Why is it that people who say they want a good relationship behave negatively towards their partner and friends? Why do so many join a gym yet never go? Why do people have that extra drink they swore they wouldn't have, or say they want to be slim yet always eat too much of the wrong food?

Perhaps it is because doing the right thing is not easy. This is a common answer, but it is usually not true. Consistently doing the wrong thing – doing things that you don't want to, or that cause you grief and a negative outcome so often – now that seems much harder to me!

So why do so many people seem to take the hard road in life? Sometimes we do the wrong thing simply because we don't know what the right thing is – perhaps we don't have the knowledge or the skill, or have never been in that situation before. Sometimes we do the wrong thing because we don't think and just react automatically out of habit. Sometimes we do the wrong thing for emotional reasons. There are – it seems – many reasons why we fail to do the right thing and limit how successful we can be. In my view all these reasons can be boiled down to one simple core factor that acts as a guide to how we need to **flex**: *coherence*.

47. Towards greater personal coherence

Earlier in the book we drew attention to the fact that many of life's struggles come from people having too many habits. And a very narrow range of strategies with which to cope with their world, meaning they're faced with situations with which they cannot cope and that leave them stressed, dissatisfied or unhappy. We talked of the need to **flex** in order to expand our personal behavioural repertoire. To have a toolbox stuffed with fully functioning coping strategies. We showed how stress afflicts people with under-filled toolboxes, or narrow repertoires. And how Do Something Different is a technique to help us to **flex**.

In this section we'd like to tell you a little more about why Do Something Different works. You can no doubt see how doing lots of new and different things breaks down the habits that run the experiencing self. And that doing something different increases a person's flexibility by creating new behaviours and thoughts that impact on the reflecting self.

But ultimately Do Something Different brings about greater coherence in the individual and aligns the two selves. Many people, as we've already mentioned, go through life saying one thing and doing another. Living one life but wishing for something else. Personal coherence is the mark of someone who has all parts of their life aligned. What they do and what they say are connected. They are not held back by habits or personal limitations, and are totally at ease with themselves and their world. Their experiencing and reflecting selves are living in harmony together. In the end the hallmarks of the incoherent person, doing one thing and saying another, disappear.

Nonetheless, incoherence seems to be part of the human condition. It affects us all in large and small ways. Here are a few everyday examples:

- Craig chooses a foreign holiday but is upset when he can't get his favourite beer and there are olives in the salad.
- Pauline says she hates living in a mess but watches TV instead of doing the housework and is permanently untidy.

- Julie was desperate for children but now that she has them she constantly complains about them and secretly prefers it when they're not around.
- Roger wears a safety helmet when cycling – then stops and has a cigarette.
- The obese Simons family wear the latest sports clothing but never exercise.
- Marty is obsessive about recycling but flies long-haul.
- Almost 50 per cent of the UK population buy fresh fruit and then throw it away.
- Carol loves watching cookery programmes but can't be bothered to prepare a meal and lives on takeaways.
- Jim has renewed his wedding vows and is sleeping with his secretary.
- Kath always tries to park as close as possible to the gym where she is going to an exercise class.
- Hayley has credit card debts and a cupboard full of dresses and shoes she's hardly ever worn.
- Sally and Richard worry about their children's health but feed them a diet of junk food.

When people are incoherent there will always be some fallout or damage. Either to the individual or to others around them. Some of the examples above may seem rather flippant, but you get the message. In reality people's incoherencies can run far deeper than just a few surface behaviours. Even the simplest of human situations are immensely complex and multi-layered. The table below shows some of the layers that are important to consider for personal coherence and integration.

48. Levels of coherence

Level	Label	Description	Self
A	Evolution	Evolutionary forces	Animal
B	Biology	Biological and genetic make-up	Animal
1	Desire	Unconscious processes and thoughts	Experiencing
2	Habit	Automatic thoughts and behaviour	Experiencing
3	Thinking	Conscious thoughts	Experiencing
4	Intention	What we mean	Experiencing
5	Saying	What we say	Experiencing
6	Doing	What we do	Experiencing
7	Memory	Feelings afterwards	Reflecting
8	Reflecting	Thinking about things	Reflecting

The table above shows the many different forces and processes that come into play with personal coherence. Coherence is at maximum when Levels 1 to 8 are acting in unison, i.e. when all are operating towards the same end. The more there are discrepancies among the different levels, the greater incoherence there will be.

What each level consists of

Levels A and B represent basic animalistic processes that may exert an influence for humans too. There are many of these, but Level A, Evolution, may include aggression, competitive tendencies, territoriality and wanting to dominate. At Level B, Biology, there would be sexual forces, maternal instincts, fear, and fight or flight reactions.

Level 1, Desire, includes some basic drives and emotions, many of which will operate at an unconscious level.

Level 2, Habit, includes many acquired or learned behaviours that have become automatic. These are easily triggered by environmental cues.

Level 3, Thinking, includes more conscious processes that are likely to shape our thinking at any time.

Level 4, Intention, describes deliberate considerations and includes reference to what we mean to do.

Level 5, Saying, refers to what we express in words.

Level 6, Doing, covers our overt actions and behaviours.

Levels 1 to 6 play a role in what we experience and how we consider and behave during events in everyday life. They make up the experiencing self.

Level 7, Memory, is the passive storage of our experiences.

Level 8, Reflecting, involves active reconsideration of our past experiences and consideration of the future.

Levels 7 and 8 together make up the reflecting self.

When we are coherent, or when a coherent event occurs, all the Levels 1 to 6 – our unconscious processes, our automatic reactions, our conscious thoughts at the time, our intentions, and what we say and do – are aligned with each other. They will also cause no tension when remembering and reflecting on what happened at the time, in Levels 7 and 8.

For example, Colin is cycling to work. He has made that choice, he wants to keep fit, and he is concerned to minimise his carbon footprint. He resolved to cycle to work more this year when he could and the weather permitted. Doing this, Colin is likely to be coherent on all levels, including when he reflects on it.

For someone else, doing the same thing may be very incoherent. Perhaps the car broke down because they did not have it serviced, or they cannot afford to drive, or they had resolved never to cycle because they just don't like it, and so on. There could be many incoherent scenarios.

These are fairly clear-cut examples. There will be many occasions, however, when our motives are not clear to ourselves, when we desire something that is at odds with our situation, or we think one thing and say another, or we act in a way that is not really what we mean. In many situations there might well be very good reason why this happens (for example, we quell an urge to buy something, or we stop ourselves doing something wrong, or we act in a certain way because we 'have to'). There are many internal struggles that people fight on a daily basis.

Does this mean we should sometimes be incoherent? Yes, to begin with, perhaps. In the longer term, however, we suggest that success and well-being depend upon coherence. When a person deliberately or unconsciously acts without coherence there will be some kind of cost in personal terms, although it may not be apparent at the time.

49. How personal coherence has consequences over time

Although we believe coherence/incoherence is revealed and perceived unconsciously as well as consciously, some of the consequences of being incoherent are not immediate. Smoking is a classic example of this. Many smokers say they are happy to smoke, but eight out of ten wish they had never started smoking.

In terms of the timeline for problems surfacing

Immediate issues include a reduction in performance on things you tackle, either problem-solving, decision-making or everyday work. This is simply because a smaller proportion of your energies will be aligned to the task at hand. You are using up valuable resources by being incoherent.

It is also likely that others will notice – either consciously or subconsciously – the lack of consistency revealed by your words and actions. This can have all sorts of negative effects on you, such as feeling stressed and failing to maintain good relationships with others. Other people detect incoherence and this may result in not getting selected for teams, or groups, or failing in promotions.

Another negative consequence, though not quite so clear to show, is that the incoherence is likely to create negative emotional and other forces within you. This might reveal itself in tension, anxieties, stress or even defensiveness and feelings of unease, especially as your cognitive system mulls over how to align those incoherences.

It is more likely that, to begin with, you will notice your own incoherences when they first emerge as feelings of unease. It is easier to do something about them at this point. However, this is often not possible because the signs are not very obvious and it may be that you do not realise what the signals are that you are getting (internally and from others).

As time goes by and you live with your own incoherences they become more firmly entrenched by the force of habit. However, people who have incoherences within Levels 3 to 5 will find life a particular struggle. At these levels the incoherences are usually felt by the person and cannot be ignored. They may try to plaster over them with self-justifying reasons and self-deceptions. For example, the recidivist smoker might say to themselves 'one won't matter', or the inveterate shopper may hide purchases from their partner and put their behaviour down to a fault in the other.

Longer-term consequences of incoherence come in many forms. In a sense, incoherence is a form of lying to yourself and will bring with it all the attendant problems of lying. This means that as time goes by the self-lying requires more and more complex processes and self-deceptions to maintain. This is likely to multiply the incoherence many times more. As this happens the incoherences that once were evident only perhaps to you become plainer for others to see (because it is not possible to hide them) and they often become more extensive and infect more aspects of you and your behaviours. This will make you a less attractive person to others in many ways, but it is also likely to make you a less attractive person to yourself too. When this happens things can easily fall apart – damaging you, psychologically and/or physically, and your life in many areas. The trouble is that even at this stage people often do not see the incoherences within themselves and cannot see in themselves what is plain to others. A fresh start (perhaps a new partner, or a new job) will not do the trick because habit will do all it can to keep them doing more of what they did before. Unless these incoherences are resolved the old issues will resurface. The Do Something Different techniques are aimed at helping people see and remove any incoherence.

50. Coherence units

Most decisions and actions we take are complex, although they may not appear so. To break this complexity down a little we might think of situations as being made up of different *units* of thought and action. So, for example, having dinner is likely to include units to do with eating, but also with travel (going to buy the food or getting to a restaurant), as well as others such as relationships (eating with people) and so on. A unit is something that has a goal or an end (eating for satiety, relationship for social function, etc.).

This means that we can describe lack of coherence as arising from two different sources:

- Incoherence *within* a unit, such as when a person says they are going to do something, apparently intend to, but then do something else. For example, a person wants to lose weight and intends to diet but cannot resist the chocolate when offered.

- Incoherence *between* units, such as when there is a clear intention for a person to diet but this is at odds with an invitation to friends for a slap-up dinner. The doing of the one unit (to do with eating) is, for many practical reasons, incompatible with the doing of the other (to do with relationships).

So, to include units within the definition, coherence is the alignment of all levels, or of all units within a complex situation, to the same goal or end.

51. Apparent and real incoherence

Earlier we suggested that incoherence always has negative consequences, although in fact it may be sensible to appear to be incoherent in certain situations or contexts. We said that being incoherent always leads to some negative outcome. This does not mean that a person would never *appear* to be incoherent. It is necessary to distinguish real incoherence from apparent incoherence. So far we have been discussing only real incoherence. Sometimes circumstances may require us to *act* in a certain way that belies our feelings: to appear to agree with a view, for example. This would not count as incoherence because it is both:

- *deliberate* and
- determined by the *goal* of the unit

For example, if your partner asks you 'Do I look good in this?' it may be coherent to say yes (even if you don't think so) because you know they are feeling particularly sensitive for some reason, or to avoid making a snap negative judgement because you recognise that your own taste needs developing.

Imagine you have accepted an important or long-standing dinner invitation from someone you've been longing to get together with. But you have also just started on a strict diet and know the meal will be a hearty one. It may still be coherent to go along and enjoy the meal, if the goal was to spend time with the person who matters to you. This isn't a lack of willpower or a weakness. The original intention to diet remains but has undergone rational reconsideration as a result of your ability to **flex**. However, if you stayed in instead and couldn't resist a pack of doughnuts you found in the cupboard that would not be coherent.

Real stage and film acting presents us with an interesting side-issue in relation to coherence and its importance in how others view the authenticity of behaviour. No one would assume, for example, that an actor taking the part of a nasty war commander was showing incoherence even if the actor were an extreme pacifist in real life.

One acting technique some directors employ is 'method acting'. In method acting the actors really try to 'live' a role in their heads and prepare with considerable emersion in the character's life, often for months. Some say that acting can look stilted unless the actor 'lives the part' so perhaps – even in acting – a different kind of coherence and incoherence can be detected. The success of salespeople who are 'natural' in their job may be that they excel in this type of ability too.

52. Why greater coherence leads to better decisions

Lack of personal coherence can lead to poor decisions and choices for various reasons. These include:

- **Emotions**. Emotions cloud logic and judgements. Reasoning powers seem to go out of the window for some people when the subject matter or conclusions involve emotionally laden outcomes. Emotions can also account for many of the flaws in thinking and reasoning that humans show.

- **Habit**. Inertia predisposes people to make the same choices they have made before instead of questioning their own choices. People may also have a stock of excuses to justify their decisions and behaviours.

- **Low levels of FIT**. A lack in any of the five inner constancies means a person is more likely to be distracted by the wrong options. A narrow behavioural repertoire means they will be insufficiently **flex**ible and lack essential behaviours.

- **Worrying about doing the right thing**. Being overly concerned about the reaction of others, or the ramifications a decision may have in other areas of life, can cloud judgement and make for poor choices.

- **Fantasies of thinking**. Some people live in a world of fantasy about themselves, their capabilities and how they behave. Fantasies obscure the best choices because they replace real information and insight with pretence. There are various kinds of fantasy that can get in the way of proper choices including:

  - **The pretend-only fantasy**. This happens when the person is not really 100 per cent committed to a goal, decision or behaviour that is necessary to obtain the optimal outcome. Their words are empty and devoid of action. So the personal incoherence is compounded.

  - **The commitment-without-expectation fantasy**. A person might show all the signs of being fully committed, but does not really believe or expect to be successful. Their low expectations are usually met.

  - **The hidden-effort fantasy**. This is a very common cause of incoherence. It is the failure to fully consider the actual effort required to reach the goal. It is a failure to take account of all the consequences of a decision. Many people will apparently commit to a goal because they do not consider the unseen costs. So the person might commit to and expect to realise a goal but is not realistic about all that is going to be necessary to actually achieve it.

- **The others'-effort fantasy**. This is a tendency to make a decision contingent upon other people instead of yourself. It is requiring others to do things to make something happen. This fantasy is very common with people who have low levels of self-responsibility.

Coherence is about knowing all aspects of yourself – both the experiencing self and the reflecting self. Have you, for example, looked forward to something (say a holiday, or a date) and found the reality of the situation was not at all as you imagined? How often have you made a purchase you later regretted? Or wanted something but not put any effort into making it happen? These are all examples of incoherence that can be avoided. We will see that DSD helps to remove these kinds of incoherence and to improve our choices.

53. Choices do get made, even if we feel we don't make them

Making the right choices is important for all of us in all aspects of living and working. 'Decision-making' is also accorded enormous attention and kudos in governmental, organisational and commercial settings. Good managers apparently do it well and company directors get remunerated for the 'size' and importance of their decisions (rather than, perhaps, how good these decisions are). Prime ministers' choices change the world.

Yes, choosing is big business. Choices matter. But it is our view that – in the main – choices or decisions are rarely hard. In fact the right choices are always clear and obvious. What can be harder is putting the right choices into practice. That is where **flex** is important.

It is clear that making the right choices in life is important. We make thousands of 'choices' every second, although only a few of these surface to greet us in conscious thought. Even fewer, if any, change what we do, because of the powerful force of the past and our habits. Decisions – and the thoughts and behaviours that result from them – fundamentally affect our emotional or inner lives, they determine our short-term behaviours and the responses we get from others, they determine our value and worth in the eyes of others too, and they shape the longer-term course of our lives.

It seems a little odd, therefore, that in the main we let many decisions just happen. That we end up somewhere, in a job, a home or even a relationship, without really 'knowing' how we got there. Or that we allow our decisions to be made for us by our habits.

We pay most decisions scant attention, even though they appear to make the difference between success and failure in our inner and outer worlds. It seems that the only times we agonise about the choices we make is when we are choosing which TV channel to watch, whether to go out, which car to buy or where to go on holiday. Most of us fiddle about with decisions in the 'middle ground' where habit in any case has the trump card. We often neither think about nor notice the many small decisions we constantly make. And we sometimes fail to question the 'big' decisions about such things as religion, the nature of the universe, whether an alternative lifestyle would be better, or what we can control and change. We remain unaware of the vast number of choices that we actually make. Perhaps we prefer not to be reminded of our responsibilities to ourselves because then we would have to choose to take the praise and the blame in equal measure.

People often feel they do not have agency in decision-making – for example, they think things are predetermined in some sense (it's in the stars, the Gods, the genes…) and that the illusion of control means we can do nothing of any importance to change material things. This is partly why the constancy of self-responsibility plays a key part in FIT Science. Self-responsibility can give us agency even when we feel we do not have it.

But this sense of a lack of agency in decisions is interesting for another reason. The choices that affect us *do* get made, even if we are not aware of them, even if we choose to ignore our role in making them, or even if they are automatic. Someone or something will decide for you if you do not decide for yourself. If you let this happen then the outcome may not be coherent for you. You may choose not to actively engage in the choices you make but that would make sense only if you are happy to put up with the consequences that follow. You may be unaware of some decisions you make, since they happen habitually or outside of awareness. It may be possible for a person who is like this to be coherent but they would be laid back and fatalistic in the extreme. They would not complain, or have desires, negative thoughts or any real conscious direction. In essence, this is rather animalistic and not taking advantage of being human. In reality, people are not like this as a whole, except perhaps in some small areas of thought or action.

54. The myth about decision-making

We want to stress two key points about decision-making in the next sections.

First, that there is a myth that cloaks decision-making. The myth is that people face many choices and that decision-making is difficult.

And second, that 'better' decision-making is really all about becoming coherent as an individual, and that can be achieved through DSD.

First, the myth that people face many choices and that decision-making is difficult. In fact, there aren't many real decisions to be made. Actually people often make a 'category error' when 'deciding' and they see choices where actually there are none. So much of what masquerades as decision-making is simply a matter of working out what kind of 'decision' is it.

We distinguish among three types of decision, or choice.

- **'Factual' choices**. The key to some decisions is grounded in the facts of the situation. If you know things, or can find them out, the right choice will be simply determined by the facts. I might be faced with the choice, for example, about whether I should go running to get some exercise. But my knee hurts and if I run I may cause damage to it. This would offset the possible benefits of the exercise. What should I do? The answer could lie in the facts. There are some injuries that it is best to rest, and some that would be unaffected. Probably only an expert or an MRI scan could tell you. So in these situations there are no difficulties in the choice; merely a need to find out the facts. In a sense, this is not really a choice at all. So, whether you should take vitamin supplements, which variety of apple tree you should plant, and where you should go on holiday, and a plethora of similar types of 'decision', may not involve choices at all.

- **'Random' choices**. These are situations in which current facts cannot arbitrate and determine what should be chosen. There may be relevant facts to be known or found out, but they can only inform the alternative choices. For example, a middle-aged woman might have a real choice about whether to have Hormone Replacement Therapy (HRT) to assist her in the menopausal years. In choices such as this there are facts that can be stacked up in favour of either decision. On the pro-HRT side might be the benefits of postponing the ageing process, improving energy levels, reducing mood swings and minimising hot flushes. On the anti-HRT side there is a possibly 'equal' weighting of facts such as avoiding the health risks associated with hormonal treatments (cancer etc.), accepting natural processes, and preferring natural alternatives. So it may seem to be a real choice but actually it's in the random category. Although it may not *feel* random, in a sense either alternative may be fine. Of course the facts may change over time and that may shift this choice out of the random category.

- **'Moral' or 'Life' choices**. There are fewer of these but they *are* real choices in the sense that facts will not arbitrate. The choices are also more pivotal than random choices. Because once made a whole host of consequential choices emanate from them. They are your values. For example, if you were to decide that being faithful to your partner was important to you, no amount of temptation or opportunity would be relevant to you or sway you to 'choose' otherwise. Life choices, as well as informing your moral position, may also include such issues as your choice of partner, your taste in art, whether you are religious, whether you choose to be self-employed or not, and so on. Those consequences will often masquerade as decision points (should you be tempted, for example) but they are not real choices themselves. Moral/life choices are the ones that shape your life, even though many people have not chosen them for themselves. They have adopted those of their parents or the society in which they live, sometimes at the cost of their own individuality or coherence. Again, choices do always get made and it's better to be the one who makes them than to be on the receiving end of them.

55. Choice/decision is illusory

So, which category does your decision belong to?

If the decision falls into the 'factual choice' category, the second step is simply to determine what the facts are, or what a representative sample of relevant facts would be. Finding out the facts is not the same as making a choice and in this category the right option will become clear from the facts; it will no longer be a question of choosing from alternative options.

If the decision to be made is a 'random' one, there is a sense in which the choice actually made is irrelevant. You could simply toss a coin and act on the outcome of the random decider. This may appear rather a strange suggestion for what are apparently real choices. But think about it a bit. Insofar as there are no worse factual consequences that come from choosing either of the alternatives, which is actually chosen does not matter. If it did matter, then the decision was actually a factual or a moral/life choice. Some people hesitate when faced with choices like this because they wrongly believe there is a right answer. It is the classic free will paradox, illustrated by Buridan's ass. The ass was both hungry and thirsty and died because he couldn't decide between a pile of hay and a bucket of water!

'Moral/life' choices get made for all sorts of reasons, including parental bias/upbringing, the influence of others, prejudice, random or erroneous thinking, preference or feelings. Despite these somewhat arbitrary influences on important matters, moral/life choices seem to remain relatively fixed in adulthood. This is understandable, perhaps, because they are accrued habitually, but rather odd when one considers the impact they can have on one's future life. These should at least be taken out and examined every now and again. They *are* alterable. And a recognition that they are not fixed can unchain an individual and leave them free to make the right choices (for them).

Of course, it is not always obvious, on the surface, what type of decision something is. And the choices might be complex. Decisions and choices that appear to revolve around 'factual' matters, for example, can have embedded morals, say, about religious or political matters. For example, should you use your vote strategically when you know the political party of your real choice stands no chance of winning? The decision will depend not only upon the facts but will also be influenced by your political views, for example. For a sensible shopper the decision to pay more for something may be a morally justified one because they are committed to buying locally, for example. Most people don't make wrong decisions, they make category errors and fail to notice what category of choice they are facing.

56. Why people get paid for making 'big decisions'

We would argue that many business and political choices – so called 'big decisions' – are often not real choices at all, but personal preferences made explicit. So, people who are paid to make such big decisions are really being paid not for the power of their decision-making prowess, but for being publicly accountable. The 'choices' they make are clearly visible, often for a long time, to many others.

People may argue against this view because there are really important and big consequences that emanate from those decisions. We do not deny the fact that choices have consequences. It is also undeniable that there is considerable uncertainty about the future. The big decision-maker cannot know what will happen next month in the stock market, or how the public will react to an event, even though they can make pretty good predictions about such things.

If the imperative of a business is to maximise shareholder value or make the most profit, then closing a factory that employs 5,000 people could be the obvious 'factual' choice (albeit one with enormous negative consequences for others). But other people will see this as unreasonable because they see it as a 'moral' choice. It is this exposure to criticism that we see as one reason for people being paid to make, and defend, big decisions. Our view is that business, like any other domain of life, needs to consider the moral and ethical dimension. In our own business life we have decided to embrace the values of 'conscious business'.

So to conclude this section, we would argue that a key aspect of choosing is about which of the categories the current 'choice' belongs to. People often get the categories very wrong.

57. DSD and decision-making

One good thing to know is that, as personal coherence develops, making decisions in the 'random' and 'moral' categories becomes much easier to get right. Decision-making is not a matter of deciding between alternatives, but about becoming coherent. Coherence is developed by learning to **flex** through DSD. Choices and decisions simply become easier and more obvious the more coherent you become.

That's because it is the *lack of coherence* that obscures the right choice.

If, for example, what you desire is at odds with what you say, or if your habits are at odds with what you want to do, or what you think does not correspond with how you feel, knowing what to decide about something will be difficult. So decisions will appear difficult when a person is incoherent. For a coherent person the 'choice' will be crystal clear.

People make their lives and their decisions difficult because of their incoherence. For example, you agree to work late on the same evening you had promised to take the kids to see a film. It appears to be a no-win situation but the 'right' decision is the one that is consistent with your moral/life choices. A coherent person is able to handle the consequences that arise where roles and choices appear to conflict.

58. Why does DSD improve decisions?

The eight coherence levels we detailed on p.119 are your

1. desires
2. habits
3. thoughts
4. intentions
5. words
6. behaviours
7. memories
8. reflections.

Things go wrong – decisions are wrong – when these eight levels are not coherent or when they appear to point to different choices. DSD provides a way of accessing each of these levels. If we carry on doing what we have always done, research shows that our desires and intentions, our thoughts and our memories, become buried and lost to us. Routines and habits can get detached from reasons and wants, as well as from the demands of a situation.

DSD is a great revealer. By exposing our habits it shows us where our behaviours need to change. The consequences of doing something different provoke new reactions and give us insight into how our thoughts get reshaped by our actions. When we switch off our autopilot DSD helps to reveal all facets of the situation and the choices we have become clearer to us. DSD allows us the opportunity to reclaim what we might have lost to the unconscious and automatised. DSD allows the reflecting self to see things in a new light, to go back in time and check if things have changed or not, in the situation and in ourselves.

Without the reality check of DSD, over time the wrong choices can begin to look as if they are the right choices. For example, one powerful psychological force is cognitive dissonance – if a person is incoherent at any level, cognitive dissonance will act to resolve the incoherence. That is, if someone acts in a way that is incoherent with their beliefs, the person will change their beliefs so they fit with their current actions. A person who believes aggression is wrong and then acts aggressively towards another may justify it to themselves by saying the other person deserved it. Cognitive dissonance, however, just papers over the cracks – if the basic incoherence remains within the self, the negative consequences will be revealed at some time in the future. It is no good reshaping our cognitions if our basic behaviours are not compatible with our real-life choices. Many smokers, for example, insist they like smoking despite the fact that they would rather not smoke. For most smokers, the power of cognitive dissonance may make them say they enjoy smoking, when a change in behaviour (i.e. giving up smoking) is the only coherent 'choice'.

59. People are not choice machines

People do not allow their choices to be determined in an entirely rational or clear-cut way. Human beings are not machines. We are incoherent and inconsistent. We don't systematically weigh up pros and cons and reach a balanced logical conclusion. We often overlook or even ignore facts we know, or allow hedonistic desires to dominate our choices. Our actions may be inconsistent with what we say, and sometimes we are left wondering why we made a particular choice or what was behind our intention. You may well have said, or heard someone say, 'I have no idea why I did that!'

It is also the case that people are not very good at understanding the 'facts' that might be relevant – or those that would be useful to help them choose between options. This is why as humans we don't do the right thing all the time, why we have unsuccessful relationships, find ourselves in problematic situations and why we don't do the things that we know are sensible or right. We aren't computers; we are hedonistic, emotional and habitual.

We would argue, however, that by **flex**ing and doing something different we can become more aware of how and why we are choosing, take responsibility for changing how we are, take the fear out of some choices, make sure we put our energies into the right things, and do so with a good conscience. If we can lasso this personal power and develop behavioural flexibility through **flex**, we can learn to make the right choices for us. And in doing so, we also reveal our human-ness too. Human beings may not be choice machines, but our ability to free ourselves from habits and learning histories is also what may distinguish us from rats, flies and worms. Sometimes we humans do need to exercise free choice, take charge of the reins and **flex**.

Becoming aware of the role incoherence and habit play in decision-making will itself dramatically improve the quality of our choices. DSD can be a powerful tool for developing free will.

60. Self-lying and self-deception

Becoming a better decision-maker (or, to be more accurate, a more coherent person) means allowing no room for self-deception. Achieving coherence as a person requires honesty to oneself. This means being open to those motives and reasons that we like to hide from ourselves. Being truthful to yourself may not be easy but if the goal is improvement and success there is no alternative. Lying to, or deceiving, oneself brings with it similar problems that lying to others does. No one doubts there can be a short-term benefit from lying, such as a passing hedonistic gain, or perhaps evading uncomfortable questions. The same is true for self-deceptions too. In the longer term, though, the lies catch up because the web of deceit has to grow to maintain the position and at some point it always breaks.

So how can we develop our own self-deception sensors if we need to do so to improve decision-making?

We might think that if we are deceiving ourselves we would know. This is often not so because the different layers involved in self-coherence can provide us with the evidence.

DSD provides the answer.

flex in action –
the coherence-rater

Understanding your coherence

The coherence-rater below will provide you with some insights about your **flex** coherence if you complete it honestly.

Simply rate each statement in terms of how strongly it generally applies to you.

The coherence-rater

1	I am surprised at how I feel after doing something I intended.	
2	I tell lies.	
3	I wish I could get away with things.	
4	I wish for, or desire, things I know I can't have.	
5	I wonder why I did something.	
6	I am surprised at things I say.	
7	I am easily influenced by other people's opinions.	
8	I don't find it easy to 'move on'.	
9	I kid myself that my behaviour is OK when it isn't.	
10	People don't react to me as I expect.	
11	I wish I had said something else.	
12	When thinking about my day I wish things had gone differently.	
13	I don't find it easy to change what I think or do.	
14	I do what comes into my head without thinking it through.	
15	I express a view I don't really hold because I think I should.	
16	I wish I could be less driven by my habits.	
17	I do things without meaning to.	
18	I do things I don't want others to know about.	
19	There are things I would rather not be reminded of.	
20	I do things that I know are not good for me.	
21	I am unable to stop myself doing something when I know I should.	
22	I am unsure of my values in some areas of my life.	
23	My habits are not really in line with what I want.	
24	I don't reflect much on things.	
25	I do things without thinking and things go wrong.	

Scoring your coherence-rater

Add up your total score. Subtract the number from 100.
This will give you a percentage **flex** coherence-rater score.

Interpreting your coherence-rater score

Coherence is at maximum when the eight levels are acting in unison. That is, when desires, habits, thoughts, intentions, what we say, what we do, our memories and our reflections are consistent, coherent and related to our higher goals.

High scores (70+)

Congratulations, you appear to be pretty coherent. Your inner life should be fairly free from struggles and problems. You have the coherence tools to make the most of things, so are your behaviours flexible and adaptable enough to make the most of life? Are you using all 100 per cent of your potential personality? Keep doing something different to extend yourself and grow as a person.

Medium scores (50–69)

Your answers suggest your emotions, thoughts and behaviours are sometimes – but not always – in line with each other, so your coherence level is in the mid-range. You've got a sound base from which to build greater coherence, and Do Something Different will help you to use more of your potential personality.

Low scores (0–49)

In common with many people, your **flex** coherence score shows there's room for improvement. Developing your coherence will make life better, as well as making a positive difference to how you feel in all situations. Using the DSD techniques in this book will help you get to a higher level of coherence and enjoy all the benefits that brings.

flex yourself – improve your coherence

Over the next few pages you'll find some simple exercises to try. They are aimed at giving you insights into your habits and, more importantly, at setting you on the road to greater personal coherence.

Coherence project 1 – tell me what you think of me

Incoherence can arise when we carry a distorted view of ourselves around with us. We rarely see ourselves the way others see us. Deep understanding of that difference can help us to develop greater coherence. So this project is to help you see yourself through other people's eyes. It is about getting a true sense of who you are, particularly how you come across, and your personal style. It will help you decide where to make changes, starting with the way you look and your physical surroundings. You'll make decisive choices, instead of drifting along or leaving things as habit has determined they will be. It's a first step to noticing how your personal view of yourself may not cohere with the way others see you. We start with the 'outer' you, because that's a relatively easy area to get to know; we'll tackle the 'inner' you in later projects.

Try this:

You are going to find out from other people one thing about you that could be improved upon. Here's an overview of what you'll do:

Step 1: Identify somebody.
Step 2: Ask them.
Step 3: Reflect on what you are told.
Step 4: Act on it.

Step 1: Identify somebody

Identify somebody who you think comes across well to others. Someone with outward confidence or personal style, whose opinion you value. This might be a close friend, someone you admire or look up to, or a member of your family.

Step 2: Ask them

Tell the person you've chosen, 'I'm looking for ways in which I can be better. Can you help me spot where I could improve?' This might mean stepping out of your comfort zone a little. You may not be used to opening up to others in this way but most people will respond very positively to being asked to help.

Go through the TELL ME ABOUT ME lists that follow here with the help of your friend. Ask them to give you information about how THEY see you (you could do the same for them if they wanted). Of course, your friend may see some things as being sensitive areas for you and won't want to offend you. Try to listen to what they say, stay neutral, resist the urge to respond and don't be defensive. Don't feel criticised or tempted to counter what they say.

Step 3: Reflect on what you are told

You don't have to believe everything you hear and only some of it may be worth acting upon. You have to decide, since these are just things for you to think about and you're not going to change everything. But you might find out just one thing that you could change for the better and that might be the catalyst for further improvements.

You could ask them to give you feedback on yourself. Use the list on p.147.

ASK FOR ONE GOOD THING ABOUT YOU IN THAT AREA AND ONE WAY IN WHICH YOU COULD IMPROVE.

Step 4: Act on it

If there are areas that after reflection you feel you should do something about, this is the time to make plans to do that.

Some changes you decide to make will be minor ones that you find quite easy to put into practice.

Other changes will need a longer-term plan of action. It might be helpful if you:

- Make sure you have clear goals for each of the areas you want to change.

- Write them down.

- Have a time plan to guide you, but make it realistic. Allow twice as much time as you think you'll need so that you don't set yourself up to fail (research shows that people often have expectations that are too high and then they are more likely to give up).

- Tell somebody. It's important that you include others in your plans to change. Perhaps after doing the above exercise with a friend you could tell them where you plan to make changes, how you will do it and when.

- Be realistic and recognise that any small changes you make are good.

The person you do this with is going to choose one of three ratings for each of the questions below, depending on how they think you're doing in that area. You might need to tell them some things they do not know about you too (e.g. health).

1 = NO CHANGE TO MAKE

2 = COULD WORK ON

3 = CHANGE SUGGESTED

Those areas rated '3' are the ones you need to give some thought to and maybe tackle first. Of course, the person making the suggestions may be wrong and there are many things they might not know about you, your wants, your feelings and how you act in other ways. But don't just dismiss what they say. Remember, they see you in ways you do not see yourself.

TELL ME ABOUT ME

- How do I look in terms of my general appearance? (e.g. hair, dress, grooming)
- How am I doing in terms of my health and well-being? (e.g. my diet, my drinking, my weight, my fitness)
- How am I doing in terms of the people I associate with? (e.g. Am I a good friend? Have I got enough or too many friends? Do I see enough of friends and family and do they give enough back?)
- How's my living space? (e.g. Am I in the best place and does it suit my style, my needs and who I am?)
- What about my hobbies and interests? (e.g. Am I active enough? Do I need new interests? Have I become boring? Am I stretching/ developing myself enough? (e.g. reading widely, taking an interest in the world))
- Tell me about my work and career? (e.g. Am I in the right job? Do I need more training or qualifications? Am I aiming high enough? Am I valued in my job? Am I putting too much into my job? Or not enough?)

What have you learned? Are there areas where you thought you were coherent but are less so? These may be your areas for growth.

Coherence project 2 – time to watch my language
What you say, and how you say it, matters.

This project is all about the language you use and the impact it can have on your life, without you even knowing it. As we have seen earlier in **flex**, we often say one thing, yet mean another, or act in a manner that is incoherent. This project is about letting go of habitual references to the past in the language we use in our everyday talking – this is often where incoherence traps lurk. If we constantly talk about the past there is a risk that our past behaviours will be triggered by the words we use.

For one day why not experiment with noticing what has crept into your language? Your words can have a profound effect on how you feel, what you do and what you think. Your language and the way you verbally frame events and feelings can affect your thoughts and behaviour in surprising ways.

The guidelines for this exercise are simple. There are just three of them:

1. Don't talk about the past.

2. Never use a negative.

3. Don't assume that what you've said has been heard.

It might be helpful if you could cajole a supportive partner or a friend to join in. You could even make it fun by keeping score. The idea is to spot the things in each other's conversation that we are asking you not to say. Just one day, or even half a day, may be enough to give you insight. Every time you say one of these it costs you one point (or token, or even pounds if you like!). Keep a running score and see who's the best at watching their language. Or do it on your own and catch yourself when you break any of these rules.

1. Don't talk about the past – make the future

It is so easy to live in the past with your language. We habitually talk about the past to justify what we think and do, even if what we say does not really match how we currently feel or our present lives. People often have a rosy view of the past, convince themselves that things aren't what they used to be, wallow in nostalgia or dwell on memories of things that have happened. But it can give them a distorted view of the present, or mean that they don't appreciate what they have in the here and now. We learn to talk about ourselves and our lives in certain ways that can become outdated because we move on. So try to:

- **Catch yourself.** Notice whenever you are talking about the past and stop yourself if you can.

- **Put it into the future tense.** Turn a thought or reference to the past into one about the future. Instead of saying that things used to be better, talk instead about how things will be better in the future. You might, for example, try having a conversation with your partner or friend in which you *never* use the past tense at all! Instead of 'I did...', 'We did...', 'You were...', 'We used to...', 'It was...', you'd use instead sentences that begin 'I shall...', 'We will...'.

Once you try this you may be surprised at how often references to the past creep into conversation. It will take some practice so you might want to begin by just outlawing one type of past reference (for example, not referring to past mistakes). Habits are, of course, merely the past repeating itself, so make sure your language isn't providing a home for your habits.

2. Drop the negative – make it positive

In every conversation that takes place today, avoid all negative words. Replace them with positive ones. Try not to use 'don't' or 'can't', 'shouldn't', 'couldn't', 'mustn't', 'won't', 'haven't'. Instead, work at littering your language with more words like 'do', 'can', 'should', could', 'must', 'will', 'have', etc.

To begin with, you may be surprised at how many times you use the negative way of putting something, rather than the positive. You might like simply to spend time monitoring what you and others say so that you can learn to 'catch yourself' being negative.

3. Check that what you've said has been heard

A lot of arguments and misunderstandings happen because we assume that the meaning of what we've said has been communicated well. Very often, it hasn't and we should make allowances for this. In fact, it may always be safe to assume that what you have said may not have been properly understood. This is not the other person's fault. It's all to do with the limitations of language.

Here's a way you can demonstrate this. Next time you and another person close to you are discussing something, perhaps a topic that often leads to an argument, try this:

- Each time one person says something the other person has to repeat back what they think they have understood.
- If they don't get it right, the first person says it again.
- Then the partner tries again to say back to them what they've heard.
- Once they have agreed, the other partner makes their point and the first person tries to state it back.

You may be surprised at what the other person *thinks* you have said! People very often 'hear' speech in a different way from what the speaker intended. Even minor differences between what one person says and what another hears can lead to huge misunderstandings. So doing this exercise will enhance your listening skills and could really improve your communications and your relationships.

Coherence project 3 – doing the right things

When we're incoherent we can spend large chunks of our life doing all sorts of things that we don't really want to do – spending time with people who make us feel bad, persisting with projects that aren't going anywhere, doing things that aren't compatible with what we want – simply because we have always done them. If you are still chair of the PTA ten years after your children have left school, you may be able to relate to this. Or if you are going to reunions with people with whom you no longer have anything in common, it may be time to reconsider. And if you're planning to get fit but are spending evenings slumped in front of the TV, your incoherence is manifest.

This project will help you prioritise and do a reality check of how you are spending your time. It will help to direct your efforts towards what you want and in that way help you become more coherent.

Many people put a lot of their energy into things that aren't important for them or that aren't giving them any satisfaction. Coherence is about deciding what your priorities are. And that may mean saying no to things that aren't important.

Efficient, coherent people minimise the time they spend on things that don't really matter. Are you spending too much time on the wrong things? Could you devote more time to the things that are compatible with the way you want to be? The first part of this project will help you decide what those important things are. The second part will kick-start you into sorting out your priorities and making time for the right things.

You may have heard the saying that 'Life is what happens while you're busy making other plans.' Is that you?

Part 1 – finding out what's important to me

Try this exercise: How would I like to be described years from now?

Imagine a time in the future when someone who knows you well is describing you to others at a party.

What would you like them to say about you? How do you want to be seen by others in the future? What types of things would you like them to highlight when they talk about you?

Fill in the blanks below. Aim high but don't have fantasies, try and stick to things that could happen to you. Remember you're looking ahead at how your life might be described by another person in the future.

I know this person called (your name here)

and s/he really is

You'd know him/her if you saw him/her because s/he looks

and always

S/he's the kind of person who

And his/her really good points are

Other people find him/her

In the last few years s/he has

> [blank field]

but his/her most significant achievement up until now is

> [blank field]

S/he always has time for

> [blank field]

S/he lives in a very   ... place

> [blank field]

which

> [blank field]

I've always admired how s/he values

> [blank field]

and has always managed to

> [blank field]

A few years ago she decided to

> [blank field]

and s/he did this by

> [blank field]

Once you've described the person you'd like to be, read it every day. This will help you to maintain the energy you need to reach your goal.

In this exercise you have described what you are aiming for in life. This is how you want to be in the future, the types of relationships you'll have and the kind of person you'll be – given your life situation. It's your ideal self, what you should be working towards and aiming for. Are you on the way there? How big is the gap between where you are and where you want to be?

Remember, to make your life coherent with your dreams you've got to be in the driving seat. The next part of this project will help you do just that.

Part 2 – getting nearer to the me I want to be
Next try to reflect upon how you've passed your time this week. This will highlight where your priorities lie and what you spend the majority of your life doing.

It's a useful exercise because we often say, 'I just don't know where the time goes', and the more habitual we become the faster life seems to fly by. You'll know after this how you do spend your time.

Here are a list of codes. Try to categorise each two-hour chunk of your day according to what you spent most of that time doing:

(HC) Household chores
(IN)   Intimacy, building a relationship
(FF)   Time spent with friends and family
(SD) Self-development
(WK) Working, earning money
(TV)   Watching TV/chilling out
(EA)   Exercise, leisure and activity
(SP)   Sleeping

Fill in each block in the table with a code for how you spend the time.

	SUN	MON	TUE	WED	THU	FRI	SAT
5 – 7am							
7 – 9							
9 – 11							
11 – 1							
1 – 3pm							
3 – 5							
5 – 7							
7 – 9							
9 – 11							

Once you've filled in the table, look back at that description of yourself in the future. Now look again at the week you've just filled in.

Colour code each block according to whether it takes you towards becoming that person you've described.

If you did anything that moves you *towards* being that person, colour the block in green.

If what you did would have no effect on you becoming who and what you want to be, so you're *standing still*, then that will be an amber block.

Any activity that *takes you away* from where you'd hope to be should be coloured in red.

Green   **MOVING FORWARD**

Amber   **STANDING STILL**

Red   **MOVING AWAY**

Remember that some things may come into two categories. Cooking, for example, could be:

- GREEN if it's baking your own bread for the first time and you're choosing to do this because you want to be the sort of person who is able to turn your hand to anything or engage in activities that will de-stress you and reconnect you with simple pleasures.
- RED if you want to be that kind of person but you heat up a ready meal.
- AMBER if you serve up your usual meal because, in terms of your goal, it's standing still.

You'll probably colour code the time you spend with your partner too. If you're aiming to be closer and communicate more in the future but your time together is spent in front of the telly that may be an AMBER or even a RED. In the next stage of this project you might plan to spend an evening over a candlelit dinner just talking. That *would* move you towards your goal and would definitely be a GREEN block.

Now look ahead and plan a week that WILL move you in the right direction.

Build things into your diary that will make a positive difference to where you are going – things that you can colour code in green.

Think carefully about all the red blocks in the table you filled in for your last week.

Try to minimise the red blocks in the week to come. Just swapping two evenings' TV watching for more productive activities or an alternative form of relaxation could make a huge difference to your life.

Aim for more green blocks and write in each what you will do. Make it coherent with the ideal self that you wrote about earlier.

You can repeat this exercise in future weeks too if you want to.

Remember your aim is to get more green blocks into your week. It may not become totally green overnight, but if you can just add one green block per week you'll be able to see how, step-by-step, you're moving towards your goal.

Here are the codes again:

(HC)	**Household chores**	**(SD)**	**Self-development**
(IN)	**Intimacy, building a relationship**	**(WK)**	**Working, earning money**
		(TV)	**Watching TV/chilling out**
(FF)	**Time spent with friends and family**	**(EA)**	**Exercise, leisure and activity**
		(SP)	**Sleeping**

	SUN	MON	TUE	WED	THU	FRI	SAT
5 – 7am							
7 – 9							
9 – 11							
11 – 1							
1 – 3pm							
3 – 5							
5 – 7							
7 – 9							
9 – 11							

4

Section 4:
Global issues and flex

61. A modest claim – flex can change the world!

One goal we have collectively is to improve the world and make it a better place where people can live happy and healthy lives. We think **flex** can help achieve this goal in all sorts of ways. **flex** can help by equipping individuals to be better people and better citizens, for example. A more powerful proposition, however, is to influence the social and political context we all live in. This is more difficult to do, but a basic tenet of **flex** makes this a real possibility. You've seen how **flex** works by increasing our range of possible behaviours in different situations. One consequence of this is that we are far better equipped to see things from the perspective of other people, and to know something about others' ways of looking at events. This is because we are more likely to understand alternative perspectives and ways of behaving, because we have become more open to them and may even have tried them ourselves. One benefit of a **flex** approach comes from the expansion and betterment of the self and from the kind of world that is a natural outcome of Do Something Different. In this section, we will look in a bit more detail at the personal and social dimensions of the **flex** approach and show you some examples of where it has dramatically changed lives.

62. Advantages of flex at a personal level

We have seen that there are many advantages for the individual of being able to **flex** and we receive testimonials every day from people who are experiencing this. We have shown why being able to **flex** makes it more likely that you could:

- *Cope more effectively in any situation and be more likely to 'do the right thing'* because of the increased behavioural toolkit **flex** gives.

- *Be less constrained by old habits,* which means greater adaptability and responsiveness in new situations and those you have not experienced before.

- *Have an enhanced level of protection against the psychological ups and downs of life that less flexible people are prey to.* Research now shows that many psychological and physical illnesses are influenced by the unconscious and conscious mind.

- *Be able to 'make it happen', whatever your goal might be,* because you have the most appropriate and effective behaviours in your repertoire.

- *See more opportunities and fewer constraints* because **flex** makes us more aware of options and alternatives. This brings with it better performance in all areas of life and relationships.

- *Become more self-actualised and therefore happier and more satisfied with life* through becoming more coherent and connected with your own needs, desires and behaviours.

- *Be more independent and tolerant of change* because you are better equipped to deal with it.

- *Be less prejudiced and intolerant of others.* One reason people become troubled by differences between themselves and others is that they are not very good at seeing things from another's perspective. The person who is able to **flex** is more psychologically pliable and can see that difference is not (usually) a threat.

- *Be better able to manage situations in life when things don't go according to expectation* because of having a flexible mind and behaviours.

- *Be more likely to employ efficient strategy management and to look more deeply at any issue* because **flex** widens perspectives and Do Something Different provides new and unexpected inputs.

- *Get noticed and cope with getting noticed.* Being able to **flex** and adapt to situations is something that others perceive as powerful behaviour.

- *Have greater emotional intelligence* because there is less chance of an emotional reaction when things don't go according to plan, or when another person acts or responds habitually instead of appropriately. **flex** also brings with it greater empathy with others thanks to enhanced understanding of self and others' needs, desires and behaviours.

- *Stop personal history repeating itself.* Flexible people are much less likely to recycle their past and make the same mistakes repeatedly. A person who can **flex** is a person who *evolves*.

- *Have a more deliberate or distinctive personal style.* The person who can **flex** is likely to be more stylish because they are more likely to do something different and try alternatives. They can also see value in difference and shun mediocrity.

63. Advantages of flex for the organisation

The individual, social and political dimensions of **flex** can be viewed in an organisational context. Organisations have a personality too – their organisational culture – and it can be just as constraining as an individual's personality. Organisations get habits, just like people. This can be even more problematic when business or market demands change.

An organisation can use **flex** in a whole range of areas where habit and entrenched culture are holding the business back. If a company is not doing very well, new ways of tackling problems are needed – they need to do something different. If an organisation needs to innovate, for example, DSD techniques will introduce fresh ideas and behaviours. Training is a common approach many organisations take to improve things. But that training usually seeks only to educate and inform. Our DSD programmes provide a different kind of solution. Managers and employees often know what they should do but their work habits mean they fail to do it – they often use only 1/10th of their management personality! DSD can be used in focused areas of the business, or to improve things across the whole organisation.

A whole corporate organisation doing something different

When we take the Do Something Different approach into organisations wanting behaviour change you won't be surprised to hear that we do things differently. For a start, people don't go on courses! One example is a very large corporate who wanted to raise staff awareness of bias and diversity. The usual way in which this is tackled is to 'educate' or 'train' people. That often means sending them on a course. Or getting them to do some e-learning. We set up 'Project Open Mind' in the organisation that called us in, because we decided that 'Bias and Workshop Training' was a title that was sure to have staff grabbing their coats and remembering an urgent dental appointment. In Project Open Mind, after people found out about their own habits and their flexibility, we sent them a surprise task to do every day. These were of simple and fun activities. Like *'Go for a coffee with a member of your team you rarely speak to'*, or *'Ask someone much older, or much younger, than you for advice on something you're working on'*, or *'Make the effort to connect with someone in your vicinity. Smile and say hello to someone you usually ignore. Speak to people you usually nod at'*, or *'Swap a skill, shortcut or tip with a colleague. Share and learn from him or her too. Pass it on.'* And people did them. Just for fun. And over a couple of weeks things began to change in the organisation. People who had previously been overlooked, or left out (perhaps because of ethnic or gender differences), got included. Managers gained a better understanding of the potential of all of their staff, not just those in their immediate radar. Colleagues connected in new ways that created different dynamics, and some of the old 'cliques' just melted away. A project that began as a simple experiment is now a key part of the organisation's staff experience every year. It brings about growth, cohesion and development. And it's different too. Because people are having such a good time doing something different they hardly even notice they're getting 'training'.

64. Advantages of flex in the social domain

flex is excellent social grease. If we were all to expand our own world a bit with **flex** and Do Something Different, we would increase the degree to which we share a common world. Many people have an inherent tendency to believe the world exists in the form in which they see it, and as if that is the only way. You will know, however, that life is multi-dimensional. How many times have you seen the same situation from a very different perspective from someone else? Have you ever let children tell you how they perceive things? What they say (and see) is often unimaginable from an adult's perspective, yet both can be talking about the same thing. The differences between two adult views may be more subtle than that between a small child and a 'grown-up', but they are no less different. This is because the world we each inhabit is – to an important degree – unique to each of us. As we grow older our perceptions often narrow more and more and our view of the world gets more particular to us. When we say we share the same planet that does not mean we see things in the same way at all. So, it is important to understand the fundamental fact that our habitual ways and personality constrain and define how things are in the world for each of us to a considerable degree. We do live in different worlds.

It is our belief that many problems we have in the world are owing to our individual egoistic ways of seeing things. We think that if people could see things as others do, there would be fewer social and global problems. The more we understand each others' world the less tension and misunderstanding there would be. Having a more common understanding among us is key to relationships of all kinds – be they romantic, work, friends, social group, community or global. Our tendency to see the world in terms of our own experience and perspective makes us tend to reject views, perspectives and people who are not 'like me'. Prejudice – or 'prejudging' – occurs because people have a narrow egocentric view of people and events.

When we use only 1/10th of our personality we limit ourselves enormously. If we can expand that self – and if others can do the same – there is far more chance that we will overlap with others and have better social relationships. We will have room in our worlds for the views and perspectives of others, we will have the ability to understand and enjoy them, and they us.

So, we think **flex** and Do Something Different could have powerful social benefits for us as human beings living on the same planet because:

- Expanding our repertoire of behaviours means we are more likely to see things from the viewpoint of other people; we will experience perspectives more like theirs. **flex** enhances social intelligence and improves the ability we have to see and use social cues to meet the needs of others.

- It is more powerful to have an experience than simply to think it through. Action is a much more potent agent for change than thought. There are many reasons for this, but one reason is that actually experiencing something means we internalise the action and we know the consequences in more detail than were we just to think about them.

- We have seen **flex** coherence bring all the personal benefits we have outlined. We have also experienced it. But greater personal coherence also cuts down the conflicting messages we send out to others. A coherent person does not say one thing and then do another. They do not have subconscious motives and agendas that can be easily misinterpreted by others. Developing greater **flex** coherence also develops people as positive role models for others.

- It is our contention that if people do come to share a more common perspective they are also more likely to pull together for the common good on issues such as global warming, global conflicts, and in responding to natural catastrophes.

The world is currently struggling with a broad range of global issues – which include an obesity crisis in the West, increasing social disparities between rich and poor, increasing demands for health and social services that outstrip capacity, greater distrust of government, a 'blame' culture, greater intolerance and extreme perspectives, a need to reduce our carbon footprint, and so on. There are many complex reasons for these issues, so how can **flex** play a positive role? By broadening perspectives and responses at the same time as developing greater self-reliance and self-responsibility. We also argue that governments will hit a brick wall when trying to solve these problems unless individuals are helped to **flex** themselves. Unfortunately, governments tend to take responsibility and growth options *away* from people, despite saying they are trying to do the opposite. Governments cannot solve the problems that have their fundamental cause at the level of the individual.

A whole community doing something different

In 2009 a visionary group of people from a borough council in the UK decided to adopt DSD as a way of improving the health and well-being of a whole community. Along with a project manager we trained over 100 people in the Do Something Different method, including health visitors, school nurses, counsellors, outreach workers and family support workers. These professionals were shown how to implement DSD in their work and they also ran DSD groups in the schools, clinics and community centres. Gradually, lives began to change. Instead of watching TV, people were taking up street dancing or managing allotments. Instead of arguing and falling out, families were cooking together and playing board games. Volunteering took off, people became more neighbourly, and gradually the folk living in the community started to live healthier and more fulfilling lives. Two years later, when the nation's obesity rates were still rising, this was the only area in the region where levels of adult and childhood obesity had fallen. We took various measurements from the people before and after DSD and the results were astonishing.

There was a marked and significant reduction in people's anxiety and depression levels. So much so that two-thirds of the people who began the programme with a clinical level of depression were no longer depressed at the end.

Not only has the mental health of the community changed for the better, but their physical health has improved after DSD too. The frequency with which people took exercise doubled, from two days up to four days per week. The participants were eating an extra portion of fruit and veg every day. Their weight went down. Of the many smokers who went on the DSD quit programme, 88 per cent were smoke-free after six weeks. And people's life satisfaction ratings, which were below average before DSD, shot up into the above-average range. People were happy or very happy with their lives after DSD. Of course, we measured people's behavioural flexibility too and this also showed dramatic improvements after doing something different.

The stories of personal transformation are even more heart-warming than the statistics. We've lost count of the number of people who told us that this DSD community programme 'changed their life', 'gave them their life back', or even 'saved my life'. Hear it in their own words on our website: www.DSD.me.

65. flex and world issues

So it's now conceivable that many of the big problems on the planet result from people being incoherent. And being unable or unwilling to **flex**. For example, many people say they believe in saving the planet but fail to recycle, or save energy, or reduce their carbon footprint. Some people say they care about people, or hold religious views consistent with being compassionate, yet behave inhumanely or even start wars.

Coherence theory gives us insights into why many public social and health policies fail. Governments target their marketing efforts by trying to persuade us to change our minds. To understand why we should behave differently. We get bombarded with more and more information, health messages, directives or statistics to convince us of the need to change. We hear about the latest research and are told what we should do for our own good. These range from consuming a set number of units of alcohol, and five portions of fruit and veg a day, to the use of low-energy bulbs. This may serve to increase what we know – although often we knew it beforehand anyway. It mainly just adds to our incoherence by making the gulf between what we know and what we do even bigger. Because education alone will never bring about behaviour change.

Incoherence also has implications for the emotional and social economy. Many important factors that profoundly affect people are hidden from the individuals themselves, or from open dialogue, for emotional and deeper psychological reasons. A society in which people are more able to be open with themselves, and to know themselves and their capabilities and responsibilities, would be one in which a more honest discussion of social and political needs could take place. We would argue that this would be a direct consequence of greater coherence and that **flex** contains the seeds of the solutions.

There are three primary reasons why the social and emotional benefits of **flex** may be important for society. First, collectively, as well as individually, people do not have insight into why they do what they do, partly because of an over-reliance on the explicit and the conscious. **flex** reveals to the individual the 'why' and the 'how' and provides solutions that go beyond the obvious. Public dialogue is enabled by people being able to use more of their personality, in the ways outlined in this book.

Second, people are not very good at considering issues dispassionately: we easily and naturally become emotionally involved in what we do and say. At an individual level this makes us more restricted and inflexible, as we have discussed. We develop habits and other automatic patterns to defend ourselves against having to consider the way things really are. Incoherence develops as a defence and people become less tolerant of ambiguity. Such tolerance is necessary for personal and organisational growth and it is our view that a lack of this can have negative consequences socially and politically too. This is because it creates an increasingly intolerant and divisive society where differences of view are demonised, instead of being embraced. Through learning to **flex**, the individual becomes more innovative, less prejudiced and narrow-minded, and the society becomes more open and tolerant

The third dimension concerns honesty. Certain things that are known to people are not said and done in public despite the good it would do and the appropriateness and relevance. This is possibly because we lack coherence as individuals and that is reflected in the wider society. For example, politicians often put a spin on their messages because the truth might be hard to swallow. Sometimes the media provides only partial truths (and sometimes untruths) instead of being informative. This partiality and lack of honesty means that the political parties, the media and the large corporates have the power to manipulate outcomes instead of being bound by true public interest.

Imagine a world in which individuals, organisations and government were more flexible and coherent. That's the world in which we would like to live.

flex in action – challenge

Here's a challenge we'd like to leave you with

What part of your life isn't bringing you the rewards you'd like? What would you like to change?

Now think about how you behave or act in all aspects of that part of your life.

Next, think about how you could behave differently. Think about how to do the opposite of what you've been doing.

Resolve to put that into action. You are going to do something different.

Try it today.

You won't look back.

Appendix

Score your answers on the habit-rater here. Add up your total.

	Please be honest. How often do you:	Always	Usually	Sometimes	Never
1	do something you said you'd give up?	3	2	1	0
2	try something you're not very good at?	0	1	2	3
3	say that life is boring?	3	2	1	0
4	sit in the same spot to watch TV or eat a meal?	3	2	1	0
5	find out about something you don't know?	0	1	2	3
6	wear the same outfit because it's easy or comfortable?	3	2	1	0
7	change your mind about a belief you hold?	0	1	2	3
8	vary where you go at lunchtimes?	0	1	2	3
9	have the same daily meals?	3	2	1	0
10	add new people to your friendship group?	0	1	2	3
11	express the same view?	3	2	1	0
12	suggest ways to make work life more interesting?	0	1	2	3
13	visit the same holiday destination?	3	2	1	0
14	try a food or drink you think you may not like?	0	1	2	3
15	socialise with people from different ethnic groups?	0	1	2	3
16	visit the same shops for regular purchases?	3	2	1	0
17	do something that others wouldn't expect of you?	0	1	2	3
18	recall negative things that people have said or done to you?	3	2	1	0
19	stand out from the crowd?	0	1	2	3
20	watch a regularly scheduled TV programme?	3	2	1	0
21	seek the opinions of different people?	0	1	2	3
22	try to stick to a routine?	3	2	1	0
23	get bothered when people change plans at the last minute?	3	2	1	0
24	choose to listen to a different kind of music?	0	1	2	3